It's Not All Blood And Guts

My amazing life as an A&E nurse

Gary J Jones CBE

Best Wishes

It's Not All Blood & Guts
My amazing life as an A&E nurse
Print edition ISBN 978-1-5272-4801-4

Published by Gary J Jones CBE

www.facebook.com/gjjonescbe.books

First edition September 2019

The names of staff, family and friends are correct.
To ensure confidentiality the names of patients
have been changed and in some cases, the individual's gender.

Printed and bound by 4edge Ltd

Front cover photo: Thurrock Gazette

It's Not All Blood and Guts

My Amazing Life as an A&E Nurse

Gary Jones CBE

Coping with a 'dead body' coming back to life...

Climbing down a slippery embankment to care for a

lorry driver trapped in his cab...

Telling a wife her husband had just died.

Gary Jones has faced many challenges in his 40 years of A&E nursing. *It's Not All Blood And Guts* charts the career of one of the UK's foremost A&E nurses.

From his early days as a hospital cadet, through to running his own consultancy, expert witness and training company, we hear some fascinating, sometimes shocking, patient stories and we travel with Gary as he heads for Canada and the USA, returning with ideas that not only transformed the care at his own hospital but also influenced A&E nursing and paramedic development across the UK.

ABOUT THE AUTHOR

Gary Jones CBE was born in Grays Essex in 1953 and trained as a nurse at the local hospital in Orsett. He has over 40 years nursing experience in emergency care. He is a Commander of the Order of the British Empire (for services to Emergency Nursing), Fellow of the Royal College of Nursing, the Florence Nightingale Foundation and Honorary Fellow Faculty of Emergency Nursing.

Gary holds a range of nursing qualifications including the Diploma in Nursing, Ophthalmic Nursing Diploma and the City & Guilds 730 Further Education Teaching & Assessing Certificate. He has many years' experience in both clinical and managerial positions. Gary has been one of the key developers of emergency nursing within the UK and has advised at national and international level on many aspects of emergency care including paramedic training, expert nursing practice and emergency care in the community.

From 1987-1995 he was Chair of the Royal College of Nursing (RCN) Accident & Emergency (A&E) Nursing Association and from 1994-1997 the Honorary Consultant Nurse Advisor in Accident & Emergency Nursing to the Chief Nursing Officer at the Department of Health (England). Following his time as chair of the A&E Association Gary became an RCN Council Member, Vice-Chair of RCN Council and in 2005, the Convener of RCN Fellows.

Apart from his time at Moorfields Eye Hospital, Gary spent his clinical career at Orsett Hospital. Leaving the NHS in 1992, he provided consultancy, expert witness and teaching services and went on to develop a very successful training and development business. Now 50 years on since he first started work as a hospital cadet he reflects on his career and life achievements.

DEDICATION

To my parents, my sister Jackie, Nan, Grandad and Aunty Eileen.
Also to some of the key players in my career:

Mrs Kathleen Longley – Red Cross Cadet Officer
Mrs Beavis - Teacher, William Edwards School
Miss Barbara Woollings - Assistant Matron, Orsett Hospital
Miss Margaret Trimble – Matron, Orsett Hospital/Chief Nursing Officer at Basildon & Thurrock District Health Authority
Miss Hannah O'Neill - Senior Nursing Officer, Orsett Hospital
Mrs June James - Senior Tutor, Hospital Cadet Course
Mr Dragan Stefanovic - Principal Tutor, South Essex School of Nursing
Mrs Joan Pearce - Tutor, Orsett Hospital
Mr Tom Bolger - Student colleague/RCN Director of Education and later RCN Assistant General Secretary
Dr Peter Ernst – Consultant, A&E Orsett Hospital
Mr Frank Gonzalez - District Nursing Officer, Basildon & Thurrock District Health Authority
Miss Brenda Lamb - Director of Nursing, Basildon & Thurrock Hospitals
Ms Kate Harmond - Nursing Officer, North East Thames RHA
Dame Yvonne Moores - Chief Nursing Officer, Department of Health

Although this book contains the story of my life and particularly my career in nursing, no one person can achieve anything without the support and enthusiasm of family, friends and colleagues. It has been my pleasure to work with some amazing health professionals and although it is impossible to list each individual, I thank you all for your contribution to my success.

Acknowledgements

Many people have helped with this book. I would particularly like to thank:

Dame Yvonne Moores, Chair, Florence Nightingale Foundation and former Chief Nursing Officer (England) for the Foreword
Janet Snell – Editor

I'm also grateful to Mary Holmes, Sally McCornack, Jill Windle, Jackie Barlex and Pete Salt for their invaluable assistance and encouragement.

FOREWORD

I first met Gary when, as Chief Nursing Officer in the Department of Health, I appointed him as my honorary consultant nurse advisor in Accident and Emergency Nursing. It was a time of great change in the NHS and he undertook a significant piece of work around identifying the state of play in our A&E Departments, which led to the increasing contribution of specialist nursing roles in this area of practice. It was also during this time that the Chief Medical Officer led the development of community emergency care to which again Gary made a major contribution and this ultimately led to the establishment of NHS direct.

Although Gary became frustrated locally in this work in the NHS, this did not stop him in his ambition of continuing to take A&E nursing forward. Through his RCN work and his own limited company he continued to ensure that patient care was at the centre of everything he did. The Queen's Award of a CBE reflects the country's appreciation of his excellent work.

This informative and inspiring memoir demonstrates the vital role of school teachers in identifying potential, even when a teenager seems to display little ambition, and how through encouragement and support an individual can flourish and succeed. This is also a vivid account, through patient stories, of how expert and compassionate nursing makes all the difference to a person's experience of the health service.

There is though a second reason why I am thrilled to be writing this foreword. It is in my role as Chair of the Florence Nightingale Foundation that I can honour a former recipient of one of our prestigious travel scholarships which Gary received in

1980 and through it brought about a major change in his own department at Orsett Hospital and across the UK. It also enabled him to become one of the pioneers of paramedic training in the UK. It was his tremendous enthusiasm, as well as his expertise, that led him to his successful tenure as chair of the RCN A&E Association.

This memoir represents a lifetime of commitment and achievement and I hope it will inspire the next and future generations of nurses.

Dame Yvonne Moores DBE
Chair of Florence Nightingale Foundation
Former Chief Nursing Officer, England, Wales, Scotland

Contents

Timeline

1953 Born in Grays, Essex → **1964** Joined Red Cross

1969 Cadet, Orsett Hospital → **1971** Nursing Auxiliary then Student Nurse, Orsett Hospital

1974 State Registered Nurse (SRN) → **1975** Opthalmic Nursing Diploma
Night Staff Nurse A&E Orsett Hospital
Chair Thurrock & Basildon RCN Branch

1976 Night Charge Nurse Orsett Hospital → **1977** Diploma in Nursing (London)
Charge Nurse, Ward 3, Orsett Hospital
Charge Nurse Orsett A&E

1978 Senior Charge Nurse A&E Orsett Hospital → **1980** Florence Nightingale Smith & Nephew Travel Scholarship

1982 Member National Paramedic Development Programme
Awarded Red Cross Voluntary Medical Services Medal → **1983** Nursing Office A&E Orsett Hospital
Awarded Red Cross Badge of Honour and life membership

1984 Further Education Teachers Certificate → **1985** Elected Public Relations Officer RCN A&E Forum
Awarded RCN 3M Health Care A&E Award
Chair Essex A&E Group

1986 Head of Nursing ➝ **1987** Elected Chair RCN
service A&E Basildon & A&E Association
Orsett Hospitals
Nursing Officer Grays Red
Cross

1989 Centre Co-Ordinator **1990** Chair North East
Grays Red Cross ➝ Thames Regional A&E Nurse
Managers Group

1992 Resigned from the
NHS and went self-employed

➝ **1994** Honorary role as
Chief Nursing Officer's
1995 Trustee Red Cross Consultant Adviser in A&E
Essex Nursing
RCN Council member Awarded North East Thames
Florence Nightingale Region RCN Merit Award
Foundation Fellowship

➝ **1997** Vice-Chair, RCN
2000 Winner Thurrock Council
Gazette Business Awards

➝ **2002** RCN Fellowship
2003 Appointed
Commander of the British
Empire (CBE) **2004 & 5** Winner, Thurrock
➝ Gazette Business Awards

2005 Convener RCN
Fellows
Fellowship Faculty of
Emergency Nursing ➝ **2007** Director Thurrock
Enterprise Agency

2017 Sale of the business
June 1st

INTRODUCTION

"I attribute my success to this - I never gave or took any excuses."

Florence Nightingale

I was just 16 years of age as I watched a pathologist cut open a human body in a room that reminded me of a scene from Sweeney Todd. At least then, the person was dead, not like the day in Accident & Emergency when the 'dead' person I was preparing for the mortuary came back to life.

For some reason these two incidents spring to mind as I wait for my cue to walk forward and meet the Prince of Wales. It is 11am on the 23rd November 2003. The Prince is standing on the dais and the National Anthem is playing. I am towards the front of the line, walking from the picture gallery to the grand ballroom. I am about to be invested as a Commander of the Most Excellent Order of the British Empire for services to emergency nursing. For me, receiving such an honour was never in my career plan, mainly because there was never a plan at all. In fact, when I was 14 and I first considered a career in a hospital, I did not even know men could be nurses.

As I arrive at the entrance to the ballroom, in front and to my left are the Prince and senior palace officials. Behind them stand

Receiving my CBE from the Prince of Wales... It felt like my whole life had led up to that moment

two Gurkha soldiers and five yeomen warders (Beefeaters). To my right is Mum, in a wheelchair, with my sister Jackie and my friend Ray immediately behind. Again, my thoughts drift back and I recall the adrenaline rush when I was waiting for a helicopter to arrive with a multiply injured patient at one of the world's most advanced trauma centres in the USA. Then there was my brief involvement with the BBC television series Casualty. It is good to know that Charlie's post as clinical nurse manager was based on my role as nursing officer at Orsett Hospital. Inevitably, my thoughts also turn to my long involvement with the Royal College of Nursing, the British Red Cross and of course my time as one of the pioneers of the development of paramedics in the UK. So many memories and so much to tell… one day I must write a book, I said to myself.

I feel a slight tap on my arm. This is the signal to move forward and stand in front of the sergeant-at-arms. For a brief second, the enormity of what is about to happen strikes me. I hear my name and so, as instructed, I advance, turn to face the Prince, bow and walk forward to stand in front of him. As the Prince hangs the insignia around my neck, he strikes up a conversation and we chat about emergency care and the NHS. But all-too soon my time is up, the Prince raises his arm, and we shake hands. As I step back, I look directly at Prince Charles and he looks straight at me. For that one moment I feel I am the only person he is interested in. I bow and walk towards the right-hand door and back into the ballroom, with palace staff congratulating me as I take my seat. It feels like my whole life has led up to this moment and the experience is part surreal, part overwhelming.

1 THE PICTURE WINDOW

The removal lorries arrived and gradually the whole department was emptied. As the last vehicle drove off, I stood in the A&E minor injuries consulting room at Orsett Hospital in Essex, looking out of the picture window across to the village bowling green. It was July 1991. So many times I have looked out of that window, first as a student nurse, then as an A&E night staff nurse, charge nurse, nursing officer and now in my current position as head of A&E nursing services. Tears welled up and as I turned, Peter (the A&E consultant) was standing in the doorway. There was a moment's silence between us then we began to reminisce about the last 14 wonderful years. All the disagreements of the past 18 months seemed to melt away. I said my goodbyes and as I took the keys back to the main office I noticed the small brass key tag engraved with the words 'Lifeboat station'. I removed it from the ring and put it in my pocket. I'd retrieved the last of my mementoes and now I could leave this building full of memories and get on and help set its replacement at Basildon on its new course.

The fate of the Accident & Emergency department at Orsett was probably sealed back in 1973 when the A&E at Basildon Hospital opened. Although it would take until 1991 for the doors to close for good, there was always a recognition that two major A&E departments eight miles apart, and serviced by the same district health authority, was not sustainable. When I first joined the department at Orsett as a student nurse, Basildon Hospital was still being built. Orsett A&E, on the other hand, had been open since 1967 and the new wards since 1968. On

Tuesday 20th May 1969, the Duchess of Kent formally opened the hospital. In her address, the Duchess said Orsett Hospital had given 250 years' service to the neighbourhood and had gradually developed to suit the needs of a changing community. It stood on its original site and this link with the past seemed to promise security for the future.

Twenty-two years later it was hard to comprehend that future was no more, but what a great department our A&E had been. We had been pioneers in both medicine and nursing and many of the nursing developments we had championed had been taken up nationally and internationally.

And there were so many stories that picture window could tell. Like the day a young lady came back to life. I could not believe my eyes, or what my fingers felt as I placed them on her carotid artery and detected a regular and full pulse.

It began one Tuesday morning when, as the A&E nursing officer, I received a call from ambulance control telling me a young patient in cardiac arrest was on the way. So we prepared the resuscitation area and summoned the arrest team. On arrival, the ambulance staff told us the young lady had swallowed a large quantity of drugs and alcohol and had been found face down in a local lake. Resuscitation had been carried out en route and once the patient was transferred to the bed, the arrest procedure continued. As was common practice, the lady was attached to a monitor/defibrillator, we put up a sodium bicarbonate 8.4% drip, gave her adrenaline, and, of course the chest compressions continued. The anaesthetist had inserted a tube into the lady's trachea (windpipe) and was ventilating using a resuscitation bag. Further drugs were administered and resuscitation continued for over one hour.

Throughout the whole procedure, the monitor continuously showed a straight line. At one stage, the medical registrar suggested taking the lady up to a ward and placing her in a warm bath while continuing resuscitation. He was concerned that the period in the cold lake had caused hypothermia. The anaesthetist, a very domineering individual, dismissed that idea out of hand and he suggested that, after one hour with no heart activity, it was time to abandon the resuscitation and declare the lady dead.

To this day, I am convinced the registrar was unhappy with that decision but bowed to the anaesthetist's pressure. At midday, the lady was declared dead and, as was normal practice, I moved her into a side room ready for the family to pay a visit. As it was a winter's day, the heating was on and the side room was warm. I do not know why I covered the lady's body with a blanket rather than a sheet, but I did. The family came and said their goodbyes and the patient notes were sent down to the coroner's officer. It only remained for the lady to be wrapped in a sheet and transported to the mortuary.

It was now 12.30pm and I should have gone to lunch half an hour earlier. I told Sister Mack I would take a short lunch break and prepare the lady's body on my return. A little later as I started the task, I lifted the blanket and heard a groan, not uncommon as gases start leaving the body. But I did notice her skin did not appear as pale as previously. Although there was no breathing, I couldn't help feeling she did not appear as dead as she had before I went to lunch. I felt compelled to check her carotid pulse and, to my disbelief, it was very strong.

I stepped from the room and summoned Sister Mack and the medical registrar saying: "Feel the carotid pulse. Tell me I'm imagining what I think I can feel." On checking the lady's pulse Mack looked shocked and crossed her chest (she was a devout Catholic). The registrar seemed to turn pale. Both agreed there was a pulse. At this stage, we started ventilation support and the cardiac monitor showed a regular heartbeat. The anaesthetist arrived and having re-intubated and ventilated, was now far less opinionated than earlier.

I sent the porter off to retrieve the notes from the coroner's officer and called one of my nursing officer colleagues (Miss Barnard). I asked her for some advice as to how I was going to explain the situation to the relatives. Fortunately, she volunteered to do it and gave some story about continuously monitoring the dead for a period. She seemed to convince the relatives that it was some sort of miracle. After admission to intensive care, the lady made a full recovery with no brain damage. For the next few weeks I insisted that all patients who died in the department were kept until it was obvious they were cold and stiff. Once common sense returned (and the staff reminded me we were not the mortuary) I allowed normal practice to resume.

* * *

A late morning telephone call from Tilbury Docks heralded a shock for the A&E day staff. When I took the call, I was told a man had been cut in half by a straddle carrier and was en route in the docks' ambulance. A straddle carrier is a very large four-wheeled vehicle that moves and stacks containers around the docks. Each wheel is higher than a human and the cab at the top of the vehicle is in the region of 30-36 feet from the ground. The man should not have been in the movement area and had been run over.

As such events had occurred in the past, I expected either a less extreme injury or someone who would be dead on arrival. I said to one of the sisters: "Just run a normal saline drip through and we'll see what else we need when he arrives." When the ambulance pulled up, I stepped in and saw a middle-aged man with an extremely pale face. I thought he was dead, yet I observed some very slow deep breaths. "Show him under the blanket" said the driver to the attendant. As he lifted the blanket, all I could see was blood, tissue, and bone. I told the crew to bring the man in. I can honestly say I do not remember walking back into the department or speaking to the sister, yet within what appeared to be seconds I had the consultant, casualty officer and other nursing staff in the accident room. The consultant Peter Ernst had a quick look at the injuries and decided to get the man onto the resuscitation trolley. The trauma I had seen below the blanket was, in fact, the left leg ripped open and thrown across the lower part of the man's body. His chest and abdomen were stoved in. As we began to lift him, Peter had hold of the left arm, but it became detached from the man's body. With the extent of the injuries it was clear life was not viable, so we made the poor chap comfortable with analgesia, and within a few minutes he was dead.

* * *

I often thought that these events, grim though they sometimes were, would make great episodes for the BBC series Casualty. My involvement in the programme came about in 1986 when I was public relations officer for the RCN A&E Forum. A few months before our annual conference the show had been transmitted for the first time. The first few episodes depicted a small group of night staff in a large urban A&E unit. Not only did the title irritate many A&E nurses (the name Casualty was dropped in 1962 in favour of Accident & Emergency) but the initial episodes did not reflect good A&E nursing. Ethel (our forum secretary) had written to the BBC producer Geraint Morris and let him know what we thought. She also indicated that if he wanted to meet real A&E nurses he should come to the conference. To our surprise, he agreed and said he would bring his writers and the show's nurse advisor.

Grasping the opportunity to influence the increasingly popular series we organised a special slot in the conference programme. Peter Salt, a charge nurse from A&E in Bristol, was Casualty's nurse advisor. Charlie Fairhead, the night charge nurse played by Derek Thompson was modelled on Peter's charge nurse position. Peter indicated this was his first insight into working with television. He explained that he was low down the pecking order of who decided what, and although he knew many of the practices shown on the programme were not accurate, he was told that was OK because it was 'drama'. He welcomed the conference session as it gave him greater leverage when on set.

Geraint the producer was also pleased and promised that the programme would better reflect A&E today and the role nurses played. He invited the forum honorary officers to the BBC studios at White City in London to go on set, watch the filming and work with the team to ensure the programme improved.

It was a fascinating experience and we took full advantage of having our photograph taken at all the key locations around the department. We met many of the cast and spoke openly about how we believed the programme could be better. At that stage, the BBC did not have long-term plans for the show so the set had to be erected in a studio each week for filming and then dismantled. Although the scenery was very flimsy and had no ceilings, and some walls were missing (so that cameras could film the action) as we walked around it was easy to believe we were in a real A&E department.

We visited again over the next couple of years, and Casualty was given a more permanent home in Bristol. The producer and writers had also decided to change from just depicting night duty to the whole 24-hour period with incidents and action during the day shift as well as at night. The production team sought advice from Peter Salt as to how Charlie could be a senior nurse manager of the department, with 24-hour responsibility, yet still be clinically involved with patients. Peter suggested they came to see me at Orsett to discuss my nursing officer role as this was exactly what they were looking for.

Writers came to visit and when the new series was broadcast, there was Charlie reflecting my role as a clinical nurse manager with 24-hour responsibility.

When the scriptwriters spoke to me about what I did they were looking for ideas for plot-lines so I suggested an incident with hydrofluoric acid. As we were well versed with this chemical, I was able to advise the writers and then check the scripts for accuracy. The episode was based on a major disaster involving the chemical. I enjoyed that one-off involvement and I will always know that my job as A&E clinical nurse manager played an important part in developing Charlie's role in what is still a very popular show.

On the set of BBC TV's Casualty: Charlie reflected my role as a clinical nurse manager with 24-hour responsibility

2 THE RED CROSS AND EMERGENCY WARD 10

The closure of Orsett's A&E department in 1991 was part of a much larger process of centralising all acute services on to the Basildon site. Sold to the public as an improvement, it was also a way of reducing overall financial costs, vital if trust status was to be achieved in 1992. How things had changed since I started working at Orsett back in 1969.

Until I was 14 I had no idea what job I wanted to do, and I cannot remember being particularly worried about it. I had chosen not to sit the 11 plus, mainly due to my poor academic record but also because many of my friends were heading for William Edwards Secondary Modern School. My sole aim was to get through the next four years and leave school at 15, as was the norm in the 1960s. Some pupils did continue on to 16 and this linked with studying for the Certificate of Secondary Education (CSEs), something I had no intention of doing at the time. However, all that changed one evening in 1967 not long after my 14th birthday.

I was watching an episode of 'Emergency Ward 10' which depicted a plane crash. The doctors and nurses from the casualty department went to the scene. They crawled through wreckage in their uniforms to save lives. Sitting in front of the television suddenly everything seemed to slot into place for me. I walked out to the kitchen and said to Mum: "I want to work in a hospital". Her reply took me totally by surprise: "You want to be a nurse." I laughed: "Men aren't nurses." "Yes they are," she responded, "you talk to your career teachers."

The idea of asking the school's career advisors, who were both sport and geography teachers, into rugby and 'manly' careers, filled me with horror. When I did build up the courage to ask, the reply was what I expected. "You don't have the academic ability to be a nurse." I was also told: "If you want to visit the hospital you'll have to go with the girls." However, the one positive suggestion they made was that I should speak to a man who helped with the school social club who was "something to do with the hospital and nursing." What I discovered when I met him was that he was the head of the nursing school at Orsett Hospital. His advice: stay on at school, get some CSEs and apply for nurse training at 18. Stay on at school? The place I hated so much? Get CSEs when every year my school report said: 'average' and in some subjects 'below average'. Could I do that?

I decided to take things one-step at a time. Step one was a visit (with the girls) to the hospital, which I found fascinating. After another visit some weeks later my enthusiasm continued to grow. Miss Woollings, the assistant matron, spotted my enthusiasm; she also recognised the visits with the girls were not ideal. She invited me to visit alone at a weekend when she was on duty. She gave me so much information and mentioned the possibility of my becoming a hospital cadet at 16. This would give me some preparation before applying to be a student nurse and allow me to continue my education at college as well as work in a variety of departments and wards in the hospital. Miss Woollings emphasised the need to stay on at school and obtain some CSEs. The decision made, I told the school I would extend my time and, as was expected from the teenagers 'staying on,' I would study for CSEs.

On the 4th September 1967, I started in the fourth year at school. Many of my friends were planning to leave at age 15 so we were no longer in the same class. I was also disappointed that some friends became more distant, mainly because, unlike those of us who were staying on, they had no studying to do and were just biding their time until July 1968 when they could leave. Still, in the B set, the form teacher for my fourth year was Mrs Beavis. This lady was one of a small number of individuals who played a major part in my development. She knew I wanted to become a hospital cadet and eventually a nurse and she could see the potential.

Early in the year, Mrs Beavis asked me to be a class prefect which boosted my confidence. I was encouraged to join the school council and before the year was out I was reading the lesson at assembly. My confidence and maturity had grown beyond all recognition. I visited Mrs Beavis many years later and gave her a copy of my first book published by Hodder & Stoughton, Learning To Care In A&E. I told her how much of my achievements were down to her because she helped me develop. I will never forget that incredible teacher and what she did for me.

Just before the summer break, a group of us went off for a geography field study trip to Edale in the high peaks of Derbyshire, the official start of the Pennine Way. We climbed 'Jacob's ladder' up onto the Kinder Scout Plateau, and while sitting with a school friend looking out into the valley below, I said: "One day, when I'm grown up, I want to come back here." It was 24 years before I returned and, having rediscovered Edale and Castleton, I now have a short break there five or six times a year. Unlike many places in the UK, hardly anything has changed since that first visit.

On 2nd September 1968, my final school year began. Unlike past years when I didn't want to return to school, this time I could not wait to get back. This was despite the fact that it would involve more studying and also the daunting CSEs. I knew I had to do fairly well in the exams if I was going to stand any chance of employment as a cadet. Mathematics was still a big problem for me but I had taken on human biology and I knew I could do well in that.

My increased confidence and maturity meant I grew into the role of a school prefect. It taught me a lot about managing people. I knew I could be good at it because of my leadership role in the Red Cross. The difference, however, was that in the Red Cross everyone was there because they wanted to be. At school, most were there because they had to be and some made it clear they were not interested in rules and regulations.

I had joined the Red Cross in 1964 when I was 11. The enrolment certificate states: "Gary Jones was enrolled a member of the British Junior Red Cross joining with others all over the world to help the sick and suffering." Our initial activities included learning the history of the Red Cross (which I found fascinating) and some simple first aid. I found that I enjoyed learning about them, very different from how I felt about school. I took my proficiency exams in first aid, nursing and health/hygiene, thus enabling me to gain my grand proficiency badge.

Over the years, Mrs Longley, the Red Cross cadet leader, would encourage us to get involved in the local community. At Christmas we would organise food parcels for the elderly and she would drive us around delivering them. We were encouraged to befriend lonely elderly people. I remember my regular visit to one man's house was like stepping into a museum from the Victorian era.

Through the Red Cross I helped at blood donor sessions. As a cadet I was not allowed in the clinical areas, so I assisted other volunteers in the kitchen making tea and washing up. Although still a cadet (adult membership started at 16 years) as I got older I did go out into the clinical area and I observed the blood donations as well as being allowed to give out the teas. I was very impressed by the adults giving their blood so when I turned 18 I became a blood donor myself.

As the end of my school life approached not only had I become a much more confident and mature teenager, I also saw my name on the awards board: the RH Saxton Memorial Award earned me a Midland Bank Gift Cheque for my service to the community. My final report indicated that I had worked extremely hard, not only for personal gain but also for the benefit of the school. It noted my "altruistic attitude"

Me at home aged 15

and said I was very well fitted for the career I wished to pursue. What a contrast to the first year's report. As for me, I knew I was a very different person. Having stayed on at school to take my CSEs I had hoped for better results. I only gained grade 1 in human biology, all the rest were grade 2 or below. However, based on my previous educational background, getting any CSEs was a major achievement.

Turning 16 in February 1969, I was eligible to join the adult Red Cross group at Grays in Essex. I also became the assistant cadet officer for the junior Red Cross group and continued to help at the blood donor sessions. The Red Cross was the organisation that provided the first aid training to the local ambulance staff. It seems unbelievable today but in 1969 ambulance staff had very little training, but they attended the local Red Cross centre to take a first aid course.

Reflecting back on my career choice I'm sure it was down to the Red Cross, watching 'Emergency Ward 10' plus my own experience of admission to hospital in 1966. This resulted from attempting the high jump and my right elbow hitting the wooden surround. I had fractured and displaced part of my elbow and I was admitted to the orthopaedic ward at Orsett for surgery. It was fascinating watching the nurses go about their work and, following the surgery, as I regained my strength, I took a walk around the grounds of the hospital. The skeleton of the new hospital block overshadowed the old buildings. Lorries were arriving with building materials and cranes dominated the skyline. Half the hospital grounds was a building site.

During the spring of 1969, I applied for the hospital cadet course. I had two interviews, one at the hospital with the matron, Miss Trimble, and the other at Thurrock Technical College with Miss Williams. The first of these went well but when I arrived at the college for my interview and was directed to a classroom as soon as Miss Williams set eyes on me she exclaimed: "You're a boy!" "Yes," I replied "who were you expecting?" "I was expecting a girl. We've never had a male cadet before," she told me. I responded that I hoped I would be the first. I assume I made a reasonable impression because on the 10th June I received a letter and contract of employment from the South Essex hospital management committee, signed by Miss Trimble, confirming my appointment as a hospital cadet. I would work 39 hours per week for the grand salary of £241 per annum.

The cadet course involved 30 weeks per year working in the hospital and 18 weeks at the college (in two blocks of nine weeks). The appointment was on the condition that I would take training for my chosen career within the South Essex group of hospitals. I was to report to Orsett Hospital at 10am on Friday 12th September when we would be shown round the hospital, fitted for a uniform and be told about the programme.

Mum, Dad and the whole family were delighted I had set foot on the first rung of my career ladder. Although Dad never said that he wished I had followed his footsteps into carpentry, I knew he would have liked me to carry on the family tradition which went back several generations. Dad built a fantastic study area in my bedroom with a very large desk, cupboards, draws and overhead lighting. It was ideal for all the studying that lay ahead.

3 THE SUMMER OF 69

The naked body lay on the post-mortem table and the pathologist started to cut into the flesh. A large incision was made from neck to pubis and then the whole body was opened up. Looking at the man's face made me feel uncomfortable as it seemed as though he was sleeping rather than dead. The smell was dreadful, and as the organs were removed, I began to feel unwell but stood my ground hoping things would improve. I remember gazing at the pathologist handling the heart, lungs, liver and stomach and placing each one on a table for further dissection. As this was a temporary mortuary no suction system was installed so fluids from the body cavity were removed using a ladle. As the ladle was filled and the fluid tipped out into the drain I felt myself becoming dizzy. I'm told I went very pale but fortunately, I was able to leave the room and did not collapse. Once recovered, I returned to the pathology department and tried to act as if nothing had happened.

Later in the wash-up room I said to my colleagues Audrey and Mrs M: "It was the smell. I was really interested in what was happening, but the smell made me feel ill and then the ladle was the final straw. I'm sure it will be OK next time". "Next time?" Audrey looked surprised. "Yes, I'm not going to be beaten," I told her.

After a few days, I was allowed to try again. This time, Audrey and Mrs M had prepared me with a handkerchief smothered in strong perfume. Fortunately, this post-mortem passed without incident, mainly because the man's scalp was covering his face (so the skull and brain could be accessed). I spent most of the time with the hanky firmly over my nose and mouth. It provoked some comments but the staff seemed impressed that I was back. I learnt a great deal about the structures of the human body and how a pathologist determines the cause of death, so for me, it was worth the initial trauma.

*   *   *

Four weeks earlier I had mounted my Raleigh and cycled the three miles from my home to Orsett. Turning into Rowley Road, I passed the blacksmith working away at the forge. Then on through the hospital gates, I pushed my bicycle through the archway, past the hospital chapel and secured it to the bicycle rack. My career in nursing and healthcare had begun.

Strangely, I remember very little of what happened that first day except that I was the only male amongst a number of female teenage cadets. We were introduced to our tutors and the key staff, uniforms were organised and we had a tour of the hospital. My clearest recollection is of the late afternoon when I was taken to my first working area, the pathology department. Starting Monday of the following week, for six weeks, I was to work in this department. I was introduced to the two ladies who ran the wash-up room, where I was going to work. Audrey and Mrs M explained the way test tubes, bottles and a whole range of other paraphernalia were cleaned by hand then put into the autoclave or hot ovens depending on the type of material and the sterility required. There was a great deal of clinical waste, especially body tissue. This was already bagged and required sterilization in the autoclave before disposal to the hospital incinerator.

Soon after that first introduction, both ladies left for home leaving me to become familiar with the room and its contents. Suddenly the bell of the hot oven started ringing. What was I to do? At that moment Mr Yallop, the department's senior staff member, appeared. "Open the oven door," he commanded. "Put the protective gloves on and take the contents out and put them on the side to cool down." This I did, my first task in the provision of healthcare.

When I started work on that Monday morning, I was very excited as I happily "clocked in." At that time, there were two distinct parts to the hospital: the new building that had recently been opened and what was left of the old hospital and workhouse. The latter included the hospital chapel, matron's office, storerooms, the linen and sewing room, hospital kitchen and some of the old wards (two were still in use for care of the elderly patients). The old casualty department had become a temporary mortuary and the former nurses' home was converted into offices and the staff dining rooms. This old part was to remain until 1972/3 when demolition began for the second phase of the new build.

The pathology department encompassed the haematology, biochemistry and bacteriology laboratories. Along with Audrey and Mrs M my job was to wash the test tubes, specimen jars and other glass containers used for tests. These days all specimen jars and pots are disposable but in 1969 reusable jars for such things as urine specimens were still made of glass and required washing and sterilisation. Another duty was regular visits to the laboratories to collect the glassware for washing. Walking the corridor and visiting each laboratory helped me to get to know the staff which was to prove very useful in my nurse training.

Fortunately, the wash-up room had external windows. As I stood washing test tube after test tube, specimen jar after specimen jar, it was good to watch the comings and goings of the hospital. Many of the consultants were older men who had been with the local hospitals for many years. Mr Kellock, one of the orthopaedic consultant surgeons (and the one who had operated on my elbow) was an ex RAF surgeon. He had the traditional handlebar moustache and drove vintage cars. He would often arrive in a vintage open top sports car wearing his flying jacket. Across the road from the hospital were the village tennis courts

Entrance to the old Orsett Hospital, 1969

The modern wing of Orsett Hospital, 1969

and bowling green and as it was early September, it was good to be able to watch the villagers playing tennis and bowls.

As I became more confident and got to know more staff members, I started to get bored with the endless washing up. I approached Mr Yallop and asked if I could spend some time in the various laboratories. As I pointed out, if I was going to be a nurse I needed to learn more than how to wash and sterilise the glassware. He agreed, so it was washing up in the morning and then the laboratories in the afternoon, starting with haematology. There I was told about blood cells and how they were counted using a grid system through the microscope. I learnt about spinning blood to enable the different components to separate. The haematology laboratory also provided the staff to collect blood specimens from patients in the wards and outpatients (venepuncture).

My next laboratory was biochemistry. Here I discovered more about blood as well as tests for urine and other body fluids. Having been shown how to test urine, one afternoon I was on my own in the laboratory and had been left to test a few specimens. I went to the cupboard for one of the testing solutions and could not remember which bottle I needed. I knew it had a very strong smell so stupidly I took the top off one bottle, went to smell it and immediately felt as though my head was going to explode. Fortunately, I recovered without harm but I realised how cautious I must be when dealing with chemicals.

This laboratory was also responsible for histology - testing tissue specimens from both living and deceased patients. Following a post-mortem, various specimens would arrive from the mortuary and it was when my curiosity got the better of me that I asked if I could go and view a post mortem.

The final laboratory was bacteriology. Here I learnt about bacteria and viruses. How adding the bacteria from the patient specimen to culture media and then creating the right environment using ovens would allow the bacteria to grow. Once identified, by placing various antibiotic patches on the culture plate, it was possible to discover which antibiotics would kill the bacteria.

* * *

My six-week allocation flew by and next was a nine-week study block at Thurrock Technical College. I cannot say I was looking forward to it as it felt like going back to school, while the hospital had made me feel very professional.

The first college block started at the end of October and because of Christmas and New Year, we continued the nine weeks allocation into January 1970. College was much more casual than school had been - the whole ethos was you work if you want to work, but if you don't, no one is going to make you.

It was different for us hospital employees as we had been sent to the college and so the easy-come easy-go attitude was not to be our way of life. Our tutors made it clear that timetables were there for a purpose and we were expected to attend classes as directed. Mrs James was our main tutor for nursing and health care as well as being the link between the hospital and the college. Much of my essential nursing skills and ethos for caring was developed in those early days through Mrs James' teaching.

Our classes varied from continuing our general education to classes designed to develop our understanding of health and nursing/social care. Visits to sewer plants, water treatment centres and abattoirs were all part of our public health curriculum. As a group, we got on well and some of us forged friendships that would last throughout our student years and beyond. In later life, many of my cadet friends married and it was great to become friends with their partners and be a guest at their weddings. More recently, I have attended some of their retirement parties!

Following the first college block, it was back to the hospital. My second place of work was the pharmacy. This allocation was for

11 weeks so I really became part of the team. The head pharmacist was Mr Bessel. There was also another pharmacist and a number of pharmacy technicians. Bert was the pharmacy porter who provided services within the department and delivered the pharmacy boxes to the wards.

My role was to assist the technicians and the porter as well as generally helping out as required. As the weeks progressed, I became more involved with the preparation of certain medications because in 1970 many everyday medicines were made in the pharmacy. While cleanliness and sterility were important, there were no sterile/clean preparation areas. Mr Bessel would make batches of creams and medicines in the general pharmacy area and it would be part of my job to bottle or tube what had been made.

One of the common medicines used throughout the hospital was magnesium trisilicate mixture, often referred to as 'mist mag trisil'. This medicine, used for indigestion, heartburn and dyspepsia, was made and bottled in the pharmacy. A very large stainless steel container with a tap at the bottom would be prepared with all the ingredients. As the preparation was mixing and getting ready for bottling, just like a chef Mr Bessel would taste the mixture and, when it passed the Bessel taste test, I would bottle the contents. One batch would fill several dozen bottles. Once bottled the mixture would be labelled and placed on the shelves ready for distribution to the wards.

Other pharmacy-made products included creams. These were mixed and then poured into a large funnel shaped container that had a pump mechanism and large spout. I would place an empty tube onto the spout, ensure the cap was on tight and then I would pump the cream into the tube. Once filled, but leaving sufficient room at the end, I would then use a closure device to bend the end of the tube over several times. Once completed an instruction label would be stuck on the tube.

The pharmacy also bottled the methylated spirit and ether for the wards and theatre. Both products were delivered to the hospital in extremely large containers, far too big and dangerous to be housed in the pharmacy. From these large containers, the methylated spirit and ether would be decanted into glass containers known as Winchester bottles containing some 2.5 litres. These bottles, when filled, would be kept in the pharmacy and either dispensed to the theatre or the contents decanted into smaller bottles for use. Within the hospital grounds was what was called a spirit store. It looked like (and probably was) an old World War II bunker. The very large containers were housed in this padlocked building and it was the job of the pharmacy porter to take the empty Winchester bottles and fill them from the larger containers. I would often help Bert in this venture.

Bearing in mind that health and safety rules were not as stringent as today, we would collect several empty Winchester bottles in our supermarket trolley and then go across to the spirit store located in the quadrangle of the old hospital. Once inside (no masks or protective clothing) we would first decant the methylated spirit. When it came to the ether, Bert always insisted on dragging the containers outside. "We mustn't decant inside, Gary, otherwise we'll be falling asleep." We would decant the ether into the Winchester bottles outside and once all our bottles were full, and the spirit store locked, we would make our way back across the grounds, bottles clinking against each other in our trolley as we went.

* * *

The staff who lived out of the hospital were allocated a locker in the staff changing areas. Every morning and late afternoon, I would go there to change and periodically I would meet a male student nurse, Tom Bolger. Tom had recently gone into nurse training and when he became a student nurse, he continued living out so we often met up. He would tell me the highs and lows of student life and he mentioned the Student Nurses Association of the Royal College of Nursing (RCN). Tom had joined and was setting up a local group. He encouraged me to join once I became a student nurse. Neither of us knew at that time how we would both come to influence the course of nursing and the RCN during our careers.

Cadets were allocated an hour's lunch break. A meal was provided free and served in the main dining room. There were two dining rooms in the old nurses' home, one for doctors and sisters/charge nurses, the other for the rest of the staff. The dining tables were laid with white linen, cutlery and glasses. Waitresses took our order from the selection on the menu.

After my 11 weeks in pharmacy, it was back to college for another nine weeks. This time visits included the public health offices and district nursing offices. In the early 1970s, these came under the local council services (later they were taken over by the NHS but now public health is back under council control). Once when visiting the district nursing service, I was surprised to see the nurse in charge sat at her desk, in full uniform, with a huge dog under the table. How things have changed.

By the time we were all ready to return to the hospital for our next allocation I had started driving lessons. I passed my test in June of that year and looked forward to purchasing my first car. On return to the hospital, I was allocated to the general office which involved a variety of duties including printing memos and general secretarial work.

One of my jobs each Monday morning was to check the clocking in cards from the previous week. I had to check entry and exit times and note any discrepancy. This was the one and only task as a cadet that I did not enjoy. In the afternoons I would collect the money from the canteens - one in outpatients and one in maternity. I enjoyed these visits as I would be able to investigate areas of the hospital I had not visited before. Both canteens were run by middle-aged ladies so as a 17-year old I was often given tea and cake and they wanted to hear about my experience as a cadet. What should have been a short period out of the office often took me an hour or more.

Some days I would be sent to the village Post Office to buy stamps. As I was leaving, the ladies in the office would often ask me to "pop in" to the butchers or other shop to get them bits and pieces. "Don't let Matron catch you doing our shopping" they would say. Often in the afternoon Miss Trimble and Miss

O'Neill would take a stroll through the village High Road just as I was heading back. If I spotted them I would hide, ducking into the nearest shop or returning to the shop I had already been in just to avoid being seen. Once they passed I would run up the High Road and hope they did not turn round.

* * *

After the summer holidays the autumn heralded in the beginning of my second year as a cadet and my GCE exams. I was allocated ward 3 – a 44-bed orthopaedic ward. At last, I was going to be in direct contact with patients and nurses. It was the only mixed sex ward in the hospital and was geographically a ward and a half. Patient allocation was strictly females in one area and males in the other area. Bathrooms and toilets were separate for males and females.

Charge nurse David Mircic ran the ward and three state enrolled nurses had worked there for many years. In fact one, Lenny, I remembered from the old orthopaedic ward when I was in the hospital with my elbow injury. These enrolled nurses were part of an older group who had been awarded enrolled nurse status due to their years of service as assistant nurses. Their state enrolled badge from the General Nursing Council had engraved on the back S.E.A.N. (State Enrolled Assistant Nurse).

As a cadet my tasks were varied. Clean linen arriving on the ward had to be stacked in the linen cupboard. Sluices needed tidying and cleaning. Food menus meant visiting every patient to go through the menu for the next day. I collected drugs from the pharmacy, took specimens to the laboratory and often sat chatting to patients, especially those with no visitors. Although I was not to carry out any nursing duties, often the nurses would engage me in simple tasks which gave me a good insight into nursing.

One insight I did not bargain for was the day a male patient asked me to destroy a diary before his wife arrived. I took the book as requested but felt I should seek guidance from a trained member of staff. When we opened the diary, it was full of pornographic photos with names and telephone numbers. When the nurse saw the contents of the diary she was appalled and it was very rapidly destroyed.

Lenny was the nurse who introduced me to Christmas Eve carol singing around the wards. Led by the deputy matron and the local Church of England vicar and Catholic priest, nurses assembled in the main dining area of the old nurses' home. All the female nurses had capes turned inside out so the red lining was on show. We all held candle lanterns which we lit and then proceeded to the maternity unit (of course singing Away in a Manger) and then on to all the main wards of the hospital. The lights of the wards were dimmed which created a peaceful atmosphere for the carol singing. The first such concert for me in 1970 was truly memorable because as we left the old nurses' home and walked across the hospital grounds towards the maternity unit, snow began to fall. It was like a scene from a Christmas card. By about 10.30pm all the carollers were back in the dining room for coffee and mince pies. This became an annual event throughout my student and qualified years.

Unfortunately, like many traditions, it had ended by the time I left in the early 1990s.

As I headed towards my 18th birthday in February I was just too young to apply for the January 1971 intake of student nurses so I had to wait until May. I had a meeting with Matron who suggested that in the meantime I could work as either a theatre technician or a nursing auxiliary. I also needed to apply for nurse training and, due to my lack of O levels, I had to take the General Nursing Council (GNC) entrance exam.

I chose the nursing auxiliary post and applied for nurse training. The GNC exam on 29th January 1971 covered a range of questions that enabled me to demonstrate a sufficient level of English, comprehension and mathematics to pass the exam. The interview with the head of the nursing school, Mr Stefanovic, went well and his parting words were: "I expect far more from my male students." I can understand the reasoning behind such a comment as men in nursing were, and still are, the minority and consequently we were always encouraged to show we were as good, if not better, than our female colleagues. I took this challenge on board and I believe I lived up to his expectations.

In February Miss O'Neill (now the acting matron), interviewed me and the following day I received a letter from her confirming my success in gaining entrance to nurse training to begin on 3rd May 1971. As agreed, the letter also confirmed I would commence a temporary role as a full-time nursing auxiliary on day duty from the 18th February. I also heard I had been fortunate to win a special prize from Thurrock Technical College for my cadet work and this was to be presented at a ceremony the following year.

I took a holiday before starting as an auxiliary and while I was off, on 15th February 1971 'Decimal Day' was declared when pounds, shillings and pence made way for the new decimal coins. When I went to Woolworths in Grays High Street, everything was labelled in both the 'old' and 'new' money. An item priced at two shillings and sixpence (2/6d) was now 12.5p. The new prices appeared so much cheaper that as time moved on and the old prices started disappearing we noticed prices began to increase. While in the new currency these increases did not appear extortionate, when converted back to old money the item was much more expensive.

With my newfound wealth (I was now heading towards the dizzy heights of earning £551 per annum) I bought my first car on 26th February 1971. It was a red Ford Popular costing £90. No radio, no seatbelts, no rear window heater or rear window wiper, no window washers on the front but it did have four wheels and a steering wheel, and I could fill the tank with petrol for £1.

My near three months on ward 3 as an auxiliary gave me the opportunity to develop essential nursing skills such as washing/ bed bathing patients, helping them with toileting, undertaking simple wound dressings as well as assisting the nurses and student nurses with a whole range of other duties. I was also responsible for keeping areas of the ward tidy, putting linen away, making beds and many other essential tasks. Much of my training from the Red Cross and my days at college as a cadet helped me settle very easily into the nursing duties expected of me.

A number of the patients on the ward were young lads of my age who had fractured the large upper bone of their leg (Femur) in motorcycle accidents. As they had to spend three months in traction, they were usually together in the same bay. The traction involved a leg splint (Thomas's splint), and a metal pin that was inserted under anaesthetic through the lower leg bone (Tibia). On to this, weights were attached and hung through pulleys at the foot end of the bed. The splint was suspended and counterbalanced by weights and pulleys on a large bed frame. Nursing care involved re-dressing the pin entry and exit sites so avoiding any infection to the bone. The large leather thigh ring of the splint required regular lubrication to keep it supple. Pressure area care was important, although as the lads were very mobile despite being literally strung up and confined to bed, they never developed sore areas to their buttocks or back.

Having four bikers in a bay created its own challenges. Smoking was still allowed in the wards (a ban did not come in until 1979 and then only in certain parts of the hospital). In the evenings visitors used to arrive with alcohol and impromptu parties would start. During the day, the patients would throw items from one bed to another, and when they missed it was the nursing staff who cleared up the mess. It was not unheard of for games to be played, usually involving lockers being tied and then pulled into the middle of the bay.

Diet was very important, as young men with a large bone to heal required plenty of protein. Breakfast consisted of cereal followed by bacon, eggs, tomatoes or beans and toast. Lunch and dinner were always three courses. All food arrived in large heated trolleys and was served by the nursing staff. Particularly at breakfast time, there was always food left over and although strictly against the rules, we staff would then have our secret breakfast sessions. Usually, in the ward kitchen or linen room, we would eat our illicit food with lookouts posted in case the assistant or deputy matron came to visit.

Elderly patients were often admitted because of falls that had resulted in fractures of the hip joint (fractured neck of femur). Although these were surgically repaired, the patients often developed chest infections, could become immobile and were at high risk of developing pressure sores. Strict two hourly pressure area care was implemented and regular linen changes all helped reduce this risk. Once in the hospital, getting home for some patients was not an option so the long process of arranging care home facilities began. Many of these elderly people waited months before a care home was available.

Other patients who required a great deal of nursing care were those on traction due to back pain. The patient would be laid flat and traction weights strapped to both legs. To stop the patient slipping down the bed, the foot end would be raised. Such a position caused difficulty with eating and drinking as well as bladder and bowel issues. The patient needed a lot of essential care, especially with personal hygiene and bed baths. Although the bed position and traction could be altered to aid pressure area care and use of the bedpan, the patient endured a very uncomfortable experience for several days or weeks.

Patients who had undergone back surgery or suffered vertebral column injury were nursed on a Stryker frame bed. This was designed to enable the patient to lie flat at all times but allowed for pressure area care and washing. The bed was made of a pipe and canvas posterior and anterior frame. The patient would be nursed lying on the posterior frame. Every two hours the anterior frame would be strapped to the front of the patient (making them like the filling of a sandwich!) and then the bed was turned and the posterior frame removed. The patient spent the next two hours lying on their front before the whole process was reversed. It certainly can't have been much fun.

4 INTO THE TUMULTUOUS 70s

Mr Brown was admitted to ward 9 having fallen from a height of about 25 feet when the crane he was driving toppled to the ground. He sustained a small wound to the head, several fractures to his pelvis and shoulder and multiple fractures of his left rib cage. In preparation for his admission to the ward at 11.50pm, I prepared the bed and had oxygen and various equipment ready for his arrival. Although at this stage Mr Brown was not considered to need ITU care, his condition was very unstable. Frequent observations were undertaken and blood transfusion commenced. The following day he became worse and due to the deterioration, he was allocated an ITU nurse. Although the hospital had an intensive care unit, in April 1972 it was being refurbished so any patient who required intensive care was allocated a specialist nurse from ITU and nursed on a general ward. Due to Mr Brown's poor breathing he was sedated and attached to a ventilation machine. When I came on duty, the ITU night sister engaged me in the care of the patient and taught me how to record the ventilator readings and how to care for such a badly injured person. Naturally, I was nervous but I found the whole experience enthralling and over several nights my knowledge and nursing skills increased beyond measure.

For me as a student nurse of just one year the experience of nursing such an ill person, and having the opportunity to provide so much of the care, enabled me to write up this experience for what was then known as patient studies. Throughout our three years training we had to undertake four practical skills and pass each one, produce a detailed patient study, undertake various written assessments and finally undertake both the written hospital exam and our state final exam.

As I had been so involved with Mr Brown from his admission until discharge, it seemed logical to use him for my patient study. I produced a very comprehensive study, so much so that Miss Joss, one of our tutors, suggested I should adapt it for publication in one of the nursing journals. I was speechless. Here I was, just into my second year of training and I had the opportunity to write for a national nursing journal. Bearing in mind my poor English results at school and college, I had my doubts. Miss Joss and the other tutorial staff supported my efforts, reading and re-reading my attempts at an article. Finally, it was ready for submission. Miss Trimble, now the chief nursing officer for our district, gave her permission, as did the consultant. To my delight, almost a year after Mr Brown was admitted I received a letter from the *Nursing Mirror* accepting my piece for publication. In the 10th August 1973 edition there was my article 'Intensive Care Following Multiple Fractures'.

My training had begun on Monday 3rd May 1971. I was one of 13 students. A few of my colleagues had been cadets but most of the class I was meeting for the first time. There was one other male student, William Lobben. Our tutor was Mrs Pearce. After introductions we were issued with our uniforms. William and I were provided with long white coats that buttoned down the right-hand side. A purple embroider label above the pen pocket indicated I was a student nurse. The females had a purple and white striped dress, white apron, large butterfly cap and a very stiff collar. For school, we were allowed to wear casual clothes.

The Class of '71

From that Monday morning, we were going to be in the school for the next nine weeks for what was called preliminary training (PTS). We would be taught anatomy and physiology, some aspects of illness and injury and how to nurse patients, with much of the emphasis on practical skill development such as bed making, bathing a patient, bed baths, moving and handling patients, diet, fluids, intravenous fluids, fluid balance and testing urine, plus many other essential nursing skills. We would visit wards with the tutor and clinical teacher to enable us to put many of these skills into practice before our first ward allocation.

We were each given a booklet that set out the syllabus of our training and also included the record of practical instruction. The majority of the skills were repeated each year and signed off. Others were one-off skills based on specific activities. It was our responsibility to get the book signed and when returning to the school for our study blocks, it would be reviewed.

As the weeks in PTS progressed, we were all scaling a very steep learning curve. Many of our nursing lessons were linked with practice in the practical room. One day early on we were learning how to change bed linen when the patient was still in the bed. After changing the bottom sheet and rolling our colleague Jackie back and forth, the other student nurse and I were ready to sit 'the patient' up in bed. Unlike today where various lifting aids and mechanical hoists are used, we had none. I think our enthusiasm overtook us and Jackie flew up the bed and suddenly her wig was over her face. As none of us knew she wore a wig, there was a burst of laughter then recognition of her embarrassment. Fortunately, Jackie took the incident in good part and explained that due to her thin hair she chose to wear a wig and had not appreciated how the force of being lifted up the bed would disrupt her hair-piece.

Ensuring fluid balance was another important nursing skill. We were shown how to record a patient's fluid intake and output. By identifying how many glasses or cups of fluid had been consumed over a given period we recorded the fluid intake. In class it appeared straightforward but once on the wards, the accuracy was often less than desired. Patients would say they had drunk "some of" a glass of juice, "some of" a cup of tea or they would have drinks brought in and then dispose of the bottle so we would have no idea how much it contained. Intravenous fluids were much easier because we knew the content of the bag or bottle so when administered it was recorded as fluid intake.

Fluid output (urine) was simply a case of pouring the urine into a measuring jug, or in the case of the male glass urinal, standing it upright and reading the amount from the measure on the glass. The challenge of measuring urine was more difficult when both urine and stool were occupying the same bedpan!

When testing urine we were fortunate that the days of using many chemicals and bunsen burners had gone. However, the urine testing strips so widely used now were in their infancy. For testing of glucose, we had to pour urine into a test tube and add a tablet that would turn the urine a range of colours depending on the amount of glucose present. For the testing of specific gravity (the amount of fluid versus solid in urine), urine was poured into a large glass tube and a float would determine the result based on how high or low the float dropped.

Bedpans were made of stainless steel and male urinals were glass. Both required cleaning in the washer then sterilisation in the autoclave. Having worked in the wash-up room of pathology I was a professional at washing such items and a dab hand with the autoclave.

Intravenous fluids came mainly in glass bottles; this required the insertion of an air inlet tube as well as the fluid giving-set into the bottle. One of our duties was to ensure the fluid administration was stopped before the giving-set was empty as air could enter the patient's vein. As IV pumps had not been introduced we were taught how to ensure IV fluids ran to time. We had to count each drop for a minute, slowing the rate or speeding it up until the correct number of drops was achieved.

As the weeks, months and years went by, it became second nature, but that first day I was checking and rechecking until I was nearly demented with counting drops of fluid.

We tried out many of the nursing procedures on each other. Feeding our fellow students enabled us to learn how to pace the procedure and what it was like to be fed. Being blindfolded and unable to see was important for our learning. The whole emphasis of PTS was to prepare us with all the essential nursing skills so as a first-year student we could become a competent member of the ward team.

As part of that preparation, we visited wards for short periods and after four weeks we spent a day on a ward. As that day progressed, we were able, under supervision, to carry out nursing procedures. Oral temperature recordings were taken by using the glass thermometer located in the small blue fluid filled tube above the bed. As the temperature was recording and the mercury inside rose, the pulse and respirations were counted.

Later in the day, the moment came for the first injection. I had practised many times on the manikin in the school but now it was for real. I was pleased the patient was complimentary after the event; another first in my career. Further visits to the ward were made on the late shift. Finally, the end of PTS came on Thursday 17th June. As a group, we bought our tutor Mrs Pierce a large bouquet of flowers as thanks for getting us all through. And we had a party.

Parties and socialising as students became a big part of our lives.

Although the majority of students lived in the hospital, a few, including myself, lived out. In my group, only two of us owned a car. We would often try to get as many people as possible in the two cars and drive out onto the fens to a pub. Although there were two pubs in the village that we used regularly, it was nice to get for a drink on the fen. As summer had arrived, barbecues in the hospital grounds were arranged and many of the social events held on a regular basis were organised by the local Royal College of Nursing Student Nurses Association (SNA). Within two days of the start of PTS, Tom Bolger had arrived and persuaded us all to join. What I had not envisaged at the time was Tom persuading me to become secretary of the group and help him and others run many of the social events.

Orsett village was isolated though there was nothing happening in the nearby towns at night anyway. Pubs closed at 10.30pm and there were no nightclubs anywhere near Orsett. Sometimes after an impromptu party, come the early hours of the morning we would all be hungry. As the car owner, I would drive to the local burger van and bring back food then drive home before getting up for an early shift the next day. Another regular event was the film shows in the social club. We would hire a popular film and charge an entrance fee, making a small profit to keep our student association going.

In 1972 a group of us decided to enter a float promoting nursing in the Thurrock carnival. A local haulage firm provided the flatbed trailer lorry and driver. Having sought permission from Miss O'Neill, we put a range of hospital equipment on the float including patient trolleys, dressing trolleys, bedpans, intravenous

Our first carnival float in 1972   Photo: Thurrock Gazette

fluid poles and many other items. We all dressed in our uniforms and, with large placards on the side of the lorry announcing we were from Orsett Hospital, we had a great afternoon.

As that first float went well we entered another in 1973. This time our theme was promoting health and hygiene and it won us third prize. In 1974, we decided on the very popular Smurfs theme (although created in 1958 the Smurfs were still very popular in the mid-1970s) and we created the National Smurf Service. The float was adorned with items from the training room in the school of nursing and we all dressed as blue Smurfs. I was Papa Smurf with a red t-shirt and a long beard made from cotton wool. At one point on the route the beard caught in my mouth and I nearly choked. With a portable tape recorder playing Smurf songs, we won first prize.

My first ward was ward 9 (male surgery). There were two wards per floor running parallel with each other. Although the shared services were centrally located, each ward had its own dressings, drug fridge and shelves with boxes of essential equipment. You did not cross an invisible boundary line and you borrowed from the other ward at your peril.

Charge nurse Broadhead ran Ward 9. Each ward had one or two staff nurses and one or two enrolled nurses plus a nursing auxiliary. There were never more than two qualified nurses on a shift and often just one. Allocation of the work to students was based on specific activities or tasks. These included full bed baths, changing bed linen and every two hours throughout the day we had to wash and dry patient pressure areas. Other duties included maintaining intravenous drips, wound dressings and preparation of patients for theatre, including pre-operative shaving for abdominal surgery from nipples to knees.

It was during this allocation that I first realised how horrendous cancer could be. The father of a school friend was admitted with what was thought to be peritonitis. Until the day of admission, he had been very well but now complained of severe abdominal pain. He went to the theatre and on return, the notes indicated it had been an 'open and close' procedure. When his abdomen was opened, the surgeon discovered such extensive cancer that the wound was closed as no treatment was possible. Within a week, my friend's father had died.

Although I should have spent more than five weeks on ward 9, as there were a number of students on the ward the allocation officer decided I should go to ward 5 (men's medical). I was told it would be better for me as there were fewer students on that ward and I would gain more experience. Ward 5 was a 30-bed medical ward and coronary care unit. Six beds immediately opposite the nursing station were for patients who had experienced heart attacks. Each bed had a heart monitor linked to a central monitor at the side of the main station. Any patient admitted with a heart attack spent at least two weeks in the ward. For the first several days they were on strict bed rest and had to have bed baths. Although on bed rest, a commode rather than bedpan was used when required as it was considered less of a strain to gently get out of bed and sit rather than try to raise and perch on a bedpan.

Like ward 9 the workbook was made out each day and as students, we were allocated a task or tasks. Although Charge Nurse Ahrens did not hold formal teaching sessions for students, like Mr Broadhead his counterpart on ward 9, the teaching and the learning for us students was integrated within our daily duties. On ward 9 when we were changing a patient dressing Mr Broadhead would inspect the wound and tell us about wound healing, what he was looking for in the wound, how infection would present. Mr Ahrens on ward 5 would often stop me in my tracks as I passed the nursing station and put an ECG or heart rhythm strip in my hand. He would ask what I made of the graph. At first, it meant nothing but as the weeks went on, with his teaching I began to notice when certain changes occurred and had some knowledge of changes that should be reported. One day I was looking at the monitor of one patient and although not knowing what the change was, I remembered Mr Ahrens telling me some weeks before that this rhythm was dangerous and could lead to the patient going into cardiac arrest. I immediately called the staff nurse who in turn summoned the doctor.

On Christmas Day 1971, I was on ward 3 and on a split shift so went on duty at 8am. The ward was only a quarter full so the morning work of washes, baths, bed making, dressings, temperatures, and blood pressures were all done in record time. All patients were geared up for Christmas celebrations and many were the young lads on traction. The traction frame above the bed was ideal for hanging festive decorations and their Christmas cards on.

For the staff, the ward office housed a fair amount of alcohol, chocolates, and food. It was also a normal part of Christmas for staff to visit the other wards and departments. During the morning, as long as sufficient staff remained on the ward, other staff went visiting. Down in the A&E department, several days before Christmas, one of the plaster technicians would begin transforming a consulting room. He created a bar and decorated the room like a pub. With appropriate stocks of alcohol, he would open on Christmas morning and it would run through Boxing Day. Nearly everyone in the hospital would visit.

With the arrival of 1972, I was back in ward 9 and it would not be long before our group returned to the nursing school and our second year would begin. Although there were long periods between the nursing school blocks, we did have to study in our own time. Work was set for us to do while we were on the wards and we had to ensure our record of practical instruction and experience was signed for every activity.

We all continued to develop our knowledge of nursing as well as disease and treatment. Much of nursing in the 1970s was focussed on illness and how we supported the patient's recovery. Medical and surgical consultants lectured on specific illness and injury. They enjoyed being part of our training and would often speak to us on the ward and without warning would ask a question expecting the correct answer, as they knew you had been to their lecture. The medical consultant would stand in the lecture theatre like an actor on the stage. We had to rehearse the congenital, inflammatory, traumatic, neoplastic and degenerative diseases. Even 48 years on, I can still recite them.

After completing the study block we all started our first night duty which was very different to working days. For the vast majority of nights, students were the total staff complement of a ward with a night sister available via the bleep system. On many wards, the staffing levels would be two students plus or minus a nursing auxiliary. Depending on the ward, some nights there was a staff nurse plus one or two students.

My first set of nights was on ward 9. At 8pm, the day charge nurse or staff nurse would verbally hand over the ward by reporting on every patient. The report was conducted at the nursing station. Once that was over, we would organise our work for the early part of the night. Patients who required regular observations or had intravenous fluids would be seen. Some would still be recovering from their operation that day. Another staff member would start changing urine bottles, recording fluid intake/output, getting patients comfortable and generally preparing for the night ahead. As many patients were several days post-operative and up and about it was accepted practice for them to make and distribute the evening drinks. (In those days a patient having had their appendix removed, or a hernia repair, would be in hospital for about seven days. For other surgery the patient could be in for 10-12 days or longer). The men looked forward to doing the drinks and three or four of them would be in the ward kitchen heating the milk and making the tea ready to take the drinks trolley around the ward. Often just before discharge, they would have recruited the next group to take over once they had left.

By around 9.30pm the night sister would arrive to review the patients and dispense the medicines. Having taken a hospital

On night duty

report from the day nursing officer, the night sister would be aware of the general workload on the ward and any patients of concern. Prior to her arrival, one of us would have placed the medicine cards of those patients prescribed drugs for 10pm on a two-shelved dressing trolley. On top of each card we placed a medicine pot. The night sister would dispense the medication from the medicine trolley into the pots and then it was our job to wheel the trolley round the ward and give out the medicines. I always had the fear that should the trolley get knocked the pots would either slide on to someone else's card or end up on the floor. Thankfully, before I had finished my student training this practice had been abandoned and a registered nurse undertook the medicine round using the medicine trolley.

Overall command of night duty was in the hands of the night nursing officer and when she was off duty a senior night sister. Mrs Stephen the night nursing officer, had strict rules and ran the hospital very efficiently. While she was often unpopular due to her rigid approach, she maintained very high standards that everyone was expected to meet. Lights on the ward were to be off by 10.30pm. If lights were still on at that time, she would appear suddenly and often no excuse was accepted. During the early hours of the morning, either Mrs Stephen or the night sister would 'do the round'. As the ward doors opened, we would stand; the female staff often wore cardigans while at the desk, and these would be removed before the arrival of the sister at the nursing station. The troops were on parade and ready for inspection. One of the two students would go on the round, torch in hand and every patient would be inspected. As we walked, questions would be asked. "Who is this patient?" "What is the diagnosis?" "What operation has this patient had?" "Explain that procedure to me."

Once 6am came, it was time for the ward to wake up. Although we did not immediately switch the lights on, we did start taking the 6am observations of those patients on four or six hourly recordings. Morning teas started around 7am provided by the ward domestic staff. Some patients who were for theatre that morning were either given a bowl for washing or directed to the bathroom. Night sister arrived to dispense the medicines in the same risky manner as had occurred the previous evening. By 8am, the ward was to be tidy and the report on each patient written. As students, we took it in turns to write the report and hand over the ward. The Kardex was the main record of nursing care; very little was written unless a great deal of care had been given. For most patients the record read the same: good night slept well.

On ward 9 we knew how the ward should look before Mr Broadhead arrived. The nursing station must be clear of any clutter. Patients should be sitting up in their beds or up and about, ready for the day ahead. All 8am observations completed and charts properly recording the results. Most importantly all cupboard doors must be closed. Just before 8am the goods lift in the clean utility room would open and out would come charge nurse Broadhead. He would go into his office, don his white coat and come to the nursing station. Day staff and I would wait. If a cupboard door was open he would make a big issue of going to the cupboard and closing it before taking the report. As he was a pipe smoker and suffered from back pain he normally performed a bit of a back exercise and then a few coughs and all was ready. I would go through every one of the 30 patients, for most reciting the written report of 'slept well'. Where more activity had occurred, it would be information of general condition, observations, whether a doctor had been called etc. Once complete I was off home.

The second year of training continued with day duty between the three main wards (9, 5 and 3) linked with blocks of further night duty. It also meant my first state final practical exam. Part A, as it was called, involved demonstrating competency in performing an aseptic dressing. This I did and so my first exam was passed.

During the second year of training I experienced other clinical nursing areas including two weeks in the special clinic (nowadays referred to as genitourinary medicine) in Tilbury plus a day out with the district nurse. Towards the end of 1972 and into 1973, I also spent three months at the local psychiatric hospital to gain an insight into mental health nursing.

The special clinic was located in a Nissan hut on the corner of the site that once housed Tilbury Hospital. The hut had two doors, one at each end. One entrance was female, the other male. A male technician looked after the male side and a part-time sister the female side. A doctor visited once a week on Wednesday.

Although the public used the facilities, it was never busy except on days when ships arrived in the docks. As a 19yr old, I found it fascinating and eye-opening to hear the stories of how people had caught one of the several common venereal diseases. Local prostitutes were a common sight around the streets of Tilbury when the ships docked. When one well-known prostitute came into the clinic and was offered a contact slip she said to the sister: "You better give me a dozen of them."

Patient examination in the clinic took the form of visually examining the man's penis for any sores or discharge. Urine was tested and a urethral swab was taken. I must admit that as I inserted the swab into the patient's urethra it made my eyes water almost as much as his. The technician would use a microscope to help with the diagnosis and appropriate antibiotics administered. Most antibiotics were large volumes injected into the patient's buttock. With the discomfort of the examination and the treatment, I often wondered if the man would repeat the unsafe activity though some clearly did as they were regulars.

The day with the district nurse was instructive. Before community care was so acute, district nursing mainly meant wound dressings, essential care of the terminally ill and administration of medicines (mainly injections) for those patients who were unable to administer themselves. An abiding memory of that day was how difficult it was to undertake an aseptic dressing in someone's house compared to the treatment room on the ward.

In mid-November 1972, I bought my second car, a Ford Capri (now considered a classic) and I experienced my first day of mental health nursing at Runwell Hospital. This was a very large psychiatric hospital made up of individual buildings. Some were secure units while others were open and patients were allowed to walk the hospital grounds. It was not uncommon to pass people on the pathway talking to themselves. Today I pass many people who seem to be talking to themselves, but rather than having a mental illness they are talking to a discreetly placed mobile phone.

My first allocation was six weeks on Rettendon ward, the admission ward run extremely efficiently by sister McKewan. After working on acute surgical and medical wards this allocation was a complete reversal of pace. Sitting talking, playing pool, going out for walks with the patients, I was not sure if this was 'real nursing'.

A major part of mental health nursing is about befriending the patient. I linked easily with a young man of a similar age to me. We often played pool together and chatted about why he had problems. Although not the whole story, it was clear that drug misuse had played a major part in his psychiatric condition. Since being in hospital, he had not used any drugs other than those prescribed. However, once allowed out into the community to work, he had re-established contact with his dealers.

One day while we were chatting by his locker, he opened a draw and I noticed a brown lump of resin partially wrapped. I asked him about it and he immediately became defensive. "It's just a bit of blow. Don't tell anyone. I trust you." I was unsure how to proceed. Did I say to him I would not tell so I could retain his trust? Or did I tell him I was going to report it and probably destroy the bond we had? I made no commitment one way or the other and later that day sought guidance from a registered nurse. The nurse suggested I record my observation in the patient's record. At the same time he would speak with the patient and explain why it was important for me to have sought guidance and that I was genuinely concerned not to lose the patient's trust. The staff nurse also discussed with the patient how his psychiatric condition had improved since being in the hospital and how a return to using drugs could lead to major problems for his health. Although the trust had been broken and we never did have the same friendship, I felt my actions were correct for the patient's long-term recovery.

* * *

Christmas Day on the ward with all the patients and staff sitting down to a full roast turkey dinner, with the wine and beer flowing, made for a very enjoyable afternoon. Unfortunately, New Year's Day was to prove less congenial as my next allocation was to the locked high dependency ward, Plashet 1. As soon as I walked into the ward, I was scared. Many of the patients were so highly dosed on medication they could not speak or walk normally. Although a pool table was in the centre of the day room very few patients were capable of playing the game. Instead, the cues were often used to hit another patient or the balls thrown at great speed across the room. At meal times, knives and forks were counted out and counted back in.

Each day a group of the more active patients would be taken across the grounds to the occupational therapy unit. Two staff would escort the small group and, on arrival, we would all be locked into a room with a large central table and chairs. Once inside we would tip a large number of washing up bottle tops onto the table. The patients would then sit and pick up a top and put the cap on the nipple. Then the closed caps would be put into a box ready for delivery to the factory that made the washing up liquid. All afternoon the patients sat quite zombie-like, undertaking this activity. When afternoon tea arrived the domestic would not enter the room. Instead, one of the two nurses would take a tray and collect the teas. One afternoon, when my colleague had gone for the teas, a patient decided to tip over the table sending all the bottle tops onto the floor. I was so cross I insisted he got down and picked them all up. To my surprise, he complied. Meanwhile all the other patients just sat seemingly oblivious to the events around them.

My final psychiatric ward was an elderly long-stay ward. One of the patients was Gilbert a tall, well-built man - very much the gentle giant. Gilbert and I would often take walks down to the town or on a Sunday attend the hospital church. As we walked, he spoke about his life and the reason why he had been in the hospital so long. Gilbert would always tell the same story. "I was in the Navy. The captain said: 'Gilbert watch for any lights on the horizon'. 'Captain, I called, there is a light'. 'That is the moon Gilbert, you're mad,' said the captain, and I ended up in here." How true the story was I have no idea but Gilbert was convinced he was mad and frequently in church, or down the town, he would suddenly shout extremely loudly: "Gilbert's mad, Gilbert's mad". Although harmless, he caused a stir in the shops and many a shopper ran as far away as possible.

By February 1973, I was back at Orsett. What a relief. It was so good to be back nursing patients on the surgical and medical wards, and I knew that as my third year approached I could look forward to theatre, A&E and children's nursing.

My second state exam was on 9th April 1973. This was the administration of medicines. Compared with today's students, we administered medicines often without registered nurse involvement. Particularly on night duty, it was common for us to add potassium to IV fluids and we regularly administered drugs and IV fluids throughout the day and night as part of our role.

I chose the medical ward for my medicines exam, as there was a larger selection of medicines. Although this meant learning about more drugs, the actions, dosages and side effects, I felt it would give me more scope with the exam. As some drugs were to be administered by injection, I was also examined on preparing the drug, correct drawing up procedure and administration. Once completed, a discussion on my exam took place and to my great delight, a pass was given. Two out of the four practical exams were now over and just five days later I was going for my third test.

This was care of one patient for a shift and during the exam, I had to demonstrate my knowledge of the patient and his medical condition. The exam included providing direct care to the patient and working with other nurses. Again, I was successful and my final practical exam was due in February the following year.

* * *

Orsett Hospital was continuing with further building work. The old wards, offices, and departments, many of which had lain dormant since I had been there, were now being bulldozed in preparation for another large ward block, offices, new kitchens, dining room and mortuary. The building that was once the nursing home and had since been used for offices and dining rooms was also to go. This large building, with a central quadrangle, had a very large tree with a preservation order. Even today, where Orsett Hospital has been replaced by private houses, the tree remains.

With the demolition of the old buildings, a part of Orsett's history was also disappearing. Buildings that were once the modern replacements for the old workhouse were now past their sell-by date and a modern fit-for-purpose development was taking their place. Where the very grand old chapel, with its stained glass windows and oak pews, once stood was now to be the home of a modern mortuary. It was said that Gertie, a cleaner who lived in the nurses' home, was one of the last babies born in the workhouse. How true this story was I do not know. It was reputed that as a baby, a child and then an adult, this hospital had been her life. Coming towards retirement, she was perhaps the very last link the hospital would have to its past.

The hospital site was not the only major redevelopment. Grays town centre and Grays south went through a major change during the early to mid 1970s. In the town centre roads, shops and houses were flattened to make way for a new shopping mall. My birthplace, the Old Vicarage, also succumbed to the bulldozers and my aunt and uncle were re-housed in March 1976. Apart from the destruction of the Carnegie Library (built in 1903) the worst violation was the total demolition of the old Grays High Street. Many buildings were in need of restoration, not demolition. Today that street could have been as well-known as Hastings Old Town in Sussex, or the Lanes of Brighton. Instead, the whole street was flattened and the sub-standard houses that replaced those iconic buildings have since had to be demolished due to continual structural problems.

Night duty came round again and this time I was on the medical ward. One event made me realise how medication can change a person's personality and turn them quite violent. An elderly gentleman had been prescribed a common sleeping tablet, Mogadon. During the early hours, this man became very confused, and despite having difficulty in walking he suddenly got out of bed and started attacking other patients. Although frail and in poor health, he appeared to have the strength of a young fit man. It took several of us to get him back into bed. Because of his breathing problems, I administered some oxygen only to discover he had a cigarette lighter under his bedclothes which he began to try to light. Fortunately, it was out of fuel and with some physical effort, I removed it from him. Eventually, he settled and remembered nothing the next morning. The next night he was prescribed a different sleeping pill.

The theatre suite at Orsett was an interesting placement although not somewhere I wished to work once qualified. As a student the initial few weeks involved being what was called 'a runner'. I was allocated to one of the four theatres and was responsible for bringing required items to the scrubbed theatre sister and, at the end of the surgery, both the sister and I counted all swabs.

After a few weeks, I was allocated to an on-call night shift. This required me to hold a bleep and sleep in the residence block. Often in the early hours of the morning, the bleep would go off and the other on-call staff and I would open the theatre ready for the emergency surgery. As students, for us this was the opportunity to 'scrub' for an operation, assisting the surgeon and being right at the patient's side. My first ever 'scrub duty' was for a patient with appendicitis.

I had memorised the names of each instrument in the general surgical pack. I knew my Spencer Wells forceps from my dissecting forceps, my McGill forceps from my toothed forceps and all the many other instruments that I would need to be ready to pass when requested. I had practised the procedure of putting on the face mask, scrubbing my hands and putting on the sterile gown and gloves. I had learned how to suction the wound correctly and to ensure the swab count was correct. With the appendix removed and the wound ready for closure, I checked that every instrument was accounted for, every needle used for internal suturing was on the needle pad and the sister and I completed the swab count. Once all was correct the surgeon could complete the closure. During my six-week allocation, I further assisted as the 'scrubbed' nurse for eight cases ranging from ear/nose/throat surgery to repair of hernias.

During my time in theatre, Mum was admitted for a hysterectomy. The morning of her operation, I was allocated the theatre at the other end of the corridor. It was a strange feeling knowing Mum was having major surgery just yards from where I was working. Later that day I was sorting the surgical specimens for the laboratory and there, in a large jar filled with formaldehyde, was Mum's uterus. I stood and looked at it thinking to myself 'that is where it all began… my first home!'

My children's allocation was at St Andrews in Billericay, recently converted from a general hospital to a specialist burns and plastic surgery hospital. The burns unit was yet to open so many of the children in the ward were suffering from burns, while others were admitted for plastic surgery. Sister Green was a young modern sister with lots of new ideas. Her approach did not always match that of the senior nursing officer who had until recently held the traditional matron's role.

While nursing on the ward, I learned a great deal about plastic surgery and particularly how many children require ongoing surgery for many years, sometimes even into adult life. I assisted children who had surgery for cleft palate, bat ears, skin grafts and removal of various growths. Some children had major skin and muscle loss to the leg. To graft such a large piece of skin and muscle with a blood supply required what was termed a cross leg flap. A large skin flap, still attached to the donor leg was grafted to the other. For several weeks, the child would be nursed with both legs joined by the skin flap and splints. When the graft was successfully achieved, the flap would be divided.

Back at Orsett on night duty, a number of surgical patients developed 'gas gangrene' - infected wounds that I associated with First World War injuries. With so many infected wounds, my night duty medicines round was very busy as all the patients with the infection required large doses of penicillin injected intramuscularly.

The injection trays were lined up at the nursing station and the night sister would dispense the vials containing dry penicillin powder ready for us students to reconstitute with water. Once in an injectable form, it was ready for administration to the patient. The large volume of the drug meant we had to inject into the patient's buttock, a technique we had all learned in nursing school. Slowly the penicillin would be injected and although the slower the injection the less pain was inflicted, many of the men still indicated how painful it was. At one stage, a quarter or more of the patients had the infection so by the time all the injections had been given it was gone midnight and we knew the whole procedure would begin again at 6am.

When I moved onto the orthopaedic ward for another set of nights, a female patient had returned from another hospital following brain surgery. She was confined to bed, however either the brain injury or surgery had stimulated her sexual desires in such a way as to make her believe that anyone approaching her wanted to have sexual intercourse with her.

As there were usually only two nurses on night duty, it was impossible for me not to provide care for this lady. Every time I entered her single room the verbal onslaught would begin and her description of what she would like to do with me was straight out of an X-rated film. She would throw all her bedclothes off, lie naked and beg me to come to her. While trying to cover her and provide nursing care, I was very aware how a wrong gesture or word could have compromised my nursing career.

About half way through my third year, I was allocated to the

Accident & Emergency department. I had been looking forward to this as it was an area I thought I might enjoy working in and I did. Although designed to accommodate patients from the Thurrock area, due to the closure of the hospital in Billericay the department was now seeing patients from the Basildon and Billericay areas.

As a third year student I was expected to assess and treat patients on both sides of the department, minor and major injuries. On most shifts, there were only two or three trained staff so the students provided most of the routine care. When allocated to minor injuries I quickly learned how to dress wounds and apply various support bandages. On the acute/resuscitation area, I assessed new arrivals, helped the patient undress and put on a gown, recorded baseline observations of respiration, pulse, blood pressure and then worked with the doctor to carry out any treatments required.

Although as students we were involved in caring for seriously ill or injured people the trained staff took the lead. Often, when we received a call from ambulance control warning us of a patient arriving in a serious condition, I would prepare the resuscitation area by opening packs, preparing intravenous fluids and making sure the main entrance doors were open. When the patient arrived, I would assist the trained nursing staff and doctors to undress the patient, record vital signs and administer treatment.

As my seven-weeks allocation progressed, I assisted in the minor theatre where the doctor would undertake such procedures as incision of abscesses and removal of foreign bodies embedded in hands, arms or legs. I would also be assisting while a patient was under general anaesthetic during the manipulation of a fractured arm or leg prior to the application of a plaster of Paris cast.

During my last allocation to ward 9, I took my fourth and final practical examination on 13th February 1974. Part D was to manage the ward for a shift period. I arrived on duty at 8am and took the night report. As was expected of the person in charge I started my ward round speaking with every patient, checking charts and updating any changes in their care. As I went around the ward, I was also ensuring all the nursing staff were actively undertaking their duties. As the morning progressed, I prepared for the consultant ward round. Mr Hamer was one of the senior surgical consultants and he often had an entourage of doctors with him. At 10am he arrived, neatly suited and wearing his bow tie, he always gave the appearance of the classic consultant from the medical films of the time. Junior doctors scurried behind as he entered the ward. I indicated to him that I was accompanying him on his round. As always, he sped from one patient to another giving his orders as we moved. It was always a challenge to keep the notes trolley moving, keep up with him and write notes on each patient as we went. Fortunately, I completed the shift without any major issues and I passed.

On ward 9 Charge Nurse Broadhead would give me the most bizarre jobs to undertake. One morning he arrived with a small pot of red paint and brush. He told me to paint the drip stand that stood by the cardiac arrest trolley. The stand was used to hook up IV fluids during an emergency and despite Mr Broadhead insisting it stayed by the arrest trolley it was often used for routine IV fluids at a patient's bed. "If it's red perhaps they [the staff] won't move it," he said as he handed me the paint pot and brush. Having completed the job, he offered some advice as to when I became a charge nurse: "Always have a screwdriver and tin of three-in-one oil in your desk - then you'll be able to do most repairs yourself!"

Although I was now feeling very confident, I still had much to learn and that became obvious one afternoon when I was in charge of ward 9. A patient returned from theatre after a major bowel operation. I read the surgical notes and instructions for postoperative care. One instruction was to connect the rectal drain to low suction. I went across to the sister of ward 10 to check how this was done. She said, "Just connect the drain to the low suction pump". On my return, I turned the normal suction equipment to low and as I was just about to connect it to the drain, the sister rushed over and stopped me. She had realised that she had not made clear I needed a specific low suction pump and not the standard high suction machine turned to low. Apparently, if I had attached the normal suction, even at a low setting, it would have caused serious injury. Not only a lesson in surgical care, but also a lesson on communication!

My final ward as a student was ward 5 (men's medical/coronary care). Having been on this ward several times throughout my training, I was pleased to be back and as a third-year student coming to the end of training, it was commonplace for me to be in charge of the ward in the evenings between 5pm-8pm. There were four consultants and each had a different regime for treating a patient suffering a 'heart attack,' stroke, respiratory problems, gastric or duodenal ulcers. So I had to know who the consultant was and what their favoured protocol was. I learned a great deal from the charge nurse, and all the trained staff and the auxiliary (Lottie) were great fun to work with.

Monday 3rd June 1974 was state finals day. Although as students, we had taken the hospital written exam and throughout our student years, we had undertaken the state practical exams, this examination would decide our fate. The state final was held over six hours, a morning paper of three hours and then another the same length in the afternoon. Each paper had seven questions and we had to answer five.

Having finished the exam, it was now a waiting game until July when the results would be published. Until then we all continued our work on our respective wards. For me, I was becoming more interested in ward management and at the same time developing my knowledge of medical and coronary care nursing. I was also thinking of the future and hopefully becoming a staff nurse.

In the 1970s, it was expected that a newly qualified nurse would stay on at the training hospital as a staff nurse for a minimum of six months. Apart from accident & emergency and theatre, which required some post-registration experience, the nurse could often choose the ward for their first staff nurse position. I was not sure which ward I wanted as I can honestly say I enjoyed all my allocations (except the last six weeks of my psychiatric secondment).

While considering my options, Mr Ahrens asked me if I would

like to remain on his medical ward as a staff nurse. I immediately said yes as I was comfortable running the shifts and felt the experience on the ward once qualified would set me up for my career in nursing. All I had to do now was pass.

On Saturday morning the 27th July 1974 I woke early. My bed was close to the window so from around 7.30am I knelt on the bed looking out for the postman. As I looked up the road, I saw him start his deliveries in our street and I watched him go to every house until he reached ours. As the envelope fell through the letterbox, I ran downstairs and, sitting on the stairs, ripped the envelope open. I gave one loud shout as I read:

Dear Sir, I have much pleasure in informing you that you have been successful in passing the Final State Examination for the part of the Register for General Nurses held in June 1974. You may apply for admission to the Register of Nurses on payment of £10.

I drove over to the hospital and met up with all my colleagues who were also celebrating their achievements. Our tutors and Mr Stefanovic were delighted with the results and wished us all well for the future. For me, it was a great achievement. Looking back to my early school days with no ambition, thinking I would never achieve much in life, to reflecting on my school exam results and wondering, despite the effort I put in during the last two years of school, if I could ever pass. Now here I was a registered nurse who could legitimately add SRN after my name, with a lifelong career ahead of me. I felt proud, and it felt good to know my parents and close family were all proud of me too.

5 "YOU WILL SINK OR SWIM..."

A large curved needle was attached to a syringe full of phenol.
Anaesthetising the sensory nerves at the back of the patient's eye
was probably the grossest procedure I encountered in the A&E
department of Moorfields Eye Hospital in London. When a
patient was suffering from a painful blind eye, the doctor, rather
than removing it, would inject phenol to block the nerves that
caused the pain. A local anaesthetic was injected first, then the
large curved needle penetrated the skin and was directed
underneath and to the back of the eye. The phenol injection
resulted in total loss of pain.

A less traumatic procedure, and one that as a nurse I undertook,
was injecting drugs under the conjunctiva of a patient's eye.
Commonly some inflammatory conditions did not always
respond to drops so an injection under the conjunctiva worked
more effectively. Having administered local anaesthetic by drops,
I would then very carefully use the needle attached to the syringe
to just penetrate the conjunctiva while ensuring I did not
penetrate the eyeball. This was a delicate procedure but the fluid
would cause a swelling and, after removal of the needle, I would
press gently on the swelling so that I could pull the upper lid
over the eye and then strap the lid closed.

As students, we had always been advised to spend at least six
months post-registration consolidating our new roles before
undertaking further training for a second registration. I had
difficulty because I did not wish to pursue children's nursing, or
mental health. I also knew at some stage in the near future I

wanted to undertake the two-year Diploma in Nursing course, but again this required me to have a second registration. So I started to investigate.

Ophthalmic nursing was not available at Orsett, yet I had always had an interest since my granddad underwent cataract surgery when I was 15. I discovered that ophthalmic nursing was a registered qualification as a diploma under the Ophthalmic Nursing Board. The six-month course was available at Moorfields Eye Hospital which dates back to 1804 and is one of the most prestigious eye hospitals in the world. In 1975 it comprised the City Road and the High Holborn sites (the latter no longer exists).

Would I ever get the chance to train there let alone obtain the diploma? After a few weeks, I decided to apply and I was interviewed in August 1974. Arriving at the hospital, I was struck by the age of the building and how it appeared to be stuck in a time warp. The main entrance from City Road was like walking into the grand lobby of a hotel. My interview was straightforward and for what I perceived as such a major step in my career, it went very smoothly. I was offered a place on the diploma course starting on Sunday 5th January 1975.

Before I knew it, the day arrived. I was met by the home sister and taken to my room on the 6th floor of the hospital. I was told this was the sister's residence and male students were allocated to this corridor because men were not allowed in the female students' residence below. I was not to use the sisters' sitting room or their kitchen.

The room was adequate with a single bed, wardrobe, sink, desk, and chair. Having unpacked, I decided to explore the hospital and as I walked the old corridors, I felt I was following in the footsteps of nursing history.

Then I took the underground to Trafalgar Square. As I admired the huge Christmas tree and its lights I reflected on how so much had happened so quickly. I had left school, become a cadet, nursing auxiliary, student nurse and staff nurse and now here I was embarking on the next phase of my career.

On Monday morning I went downstairs to the school of nursing and met other students starting the course. There were two other men (Lindsey and Bob) and we discovered that we were next-door neighbours on the sisters' corridor. Others lived in the High Holborn branch of the hospital. Their residence was a new-build, rented to the hospital, and there were many complaints, including the lack of sink and bath plugs!

Our group was like a mini United Nations with some colleagues sponsored by their home countries. Similar to my student training, the first couple of weeks were in the school of nursing learning the basics of eye care and then on to our allocated wards. Although on the course as students, we were employed as staff nurses in ophthalmology. Although each ward had a sister or charge nurse, the majority of registered nurses in the wards were nurses undertaking the ophthalmic course.

I started on a general ward providing care for a whole range of ophthalmic conditions. A patient for cataract surgery would be admitted the day before. On the day of surgery, eye drops would be administered prior to theatre. Following surgery the patient had to lie still until the following day. The next morning the first dressing would be performed and as the nurse undertaking this procedure, I would remove the pad, clean the eyelids and inspect the eye. Although red from the surgery, the cornea should be clear and a small air bubble should be present in the anterior chamber (the front chamber of the eye). Antibiotic and pupil dilating drugs were administered and if I was happy with the eye then a pad and shield were applied and the patient was allowed to sit by the bed. This process was repeated for several days until discharge. It was very different from today where cataract surgery is a short stay procedure. When on evening duty it was common for us to be the only registered nurse on the ward and early into the course I was left in charge of an evening shift, hoping no ophthalmic emergency occurred. If it had my lack of knowledge would have become apparent.

One of the key differences working in a world-renowned hospital was that many of the eye conditions I encountered as routine were in fact extremely rare. Many patients came from countries where ophthalmic care was not to the same standard as Moorfields. It was common on any ward to have a number of patients suffering from eye conditions that related to extremes of weather or environment. Nursing some of these patients was challenging because of language barriers and cultural differences.

Like my student nurse training at Orsett, I could not simply accept what I was told, I always needed to investigate further. During a lecture on eyelid problems, a specific muscle was mentioned. Muller's muscle helps to raise the upper eyelid. I cannot remember the circumstances behind my obsession to know more about this muscle but it was not mentioned in any of the general ophthalmic books available in the library. In my pursuit of knowledge and to the shock of some of my colleagues, I went to a bookshop and bought a copy of Gray's anatomy. This book was, and still is, one of the foremost anatomy texts in the world. It cost me almost a week's wages and although I found the information I wanted on page 1124 of a book with 1471 pages, it was probably the most ridiculous thing I have ever done in my nursing career. I still have the book today (thirty-fifth edition 1973) and often smile at that impulsive purchase.

My allocation to the A&E department at High Holborn was illuminating. Having worked as a student in a general A&E department during my training, now to work in a unit dedicated to eye emergencies made me appreciate the parallels between the two. Closed angle glaucoma, where the fluid inside the eye builds up causing massive pressure inside the eye, is one of the ophthalmic emergencies we dealt with. It is normally due to dilation of the pupil causing the iris to block the drainage of the fluid. In London, when there is a sudden loss of power on the Underground, this would cause everyone's pupils to dilate. If a person was predisposed to closed angle glaucoma then the dilation of the pupil would prompt an emergency. The patient would come in complaining of extreme pain in the eye, loss of vision and often feeling very sick. If the pressure in the eye was not relieved quickly, permanent damage and loss of sight could occur. Treatment was with intensive eye drops to reduce the size of the pupil and other medication to reduce the fluid within the eye itself. Literally every minute counted and as the nurse, my role was to ensure the eye drops were instilled as prescribed and the other medication administered.

Allergy of the eyelids and eyes was a common occurrence and many a famous actor from a West End show would come into the department with a reaction to the make-up. Some were very demanding and appeared to think they were the most important person in the department, while others were very polite and recognised that although a famous West End star, they were also one of many patients to be seen.

My allocation to the operating theatre in City Road involved assisting in the operating room and it took me back to my cadet days in pathology. The theatre had its own sterile supply, so part of our work was washing, sterilizing and assembling the theatre packs. We also prepared some of the fine sutures for corneal grafts. Looking through a magnifying lens, I would take a length of suture material that was thinner than a hair and thread it through the eye of an extremely small needle. Doing this several times would become very tedious and hard on my vision.

As students, we often held impromptu parties in the High Holborn residence and this meant me walking back to City Road afterwards. In 1975 London streets were much quieter at 3am than they are today. I would often be the only pedestrian and very few cars would pass by. But turning into Charterhouse Street suddenly night turned into day. The activity at Smithfield meat market was incredible. The lights blazed and huge refrigerated lorries lined up next to the market. The local pubs and cafes were open and the whole area was bustling. As I left the market area, night reappeared and I was once again the lone pedestrian. During that journey, I would often sing (poorly) Streets of London, the popular 1974 Ralph McTell song. Even today when I hear that song played on the radio I'm catapulted back to that 22-year-old lad walking through the empty city streets in the early hours of the morning.

Knowing that I would hopefully undertake the Diploma in Nursing after my ophthalmic course I realised I still had to pass English O level so I enrolled at a local city college to continue my studies. In June of that year my persistence paid off and I achieved my goal.

While visiting my parents in Essex on Friday 28th February 1975 I saw on the television news that an Underground train had ploughed into an end tunnel at Moorgate station killing 43 people and injuring many more. This was the worst disaster the London Underground system had encountered. The rescue efforts took all weekend and when I returned to Moorgate station on the Sunday evening most of it was closed. Walking up the stairs I passed large fresh air tubes running from the surface down onto the platform and into the wrecked train. Due to the risk of infection from the bodies still trapped in the wreckage large rectangular disinfectant pools were strategically placed around the station entrances. All rescuers wore boots and protective clothing and many donned masks to avoid airborne contamination. The station was a disaster zone and a very different scene to the one I had left only two nights previously.

Although six months seemed a long time, July was suddenly upon us and that meant the hospital and the board exams. Fortunately I passed both, receiving my Moorfields Diploma and Cross on 5th July 1975 and my Ophthalmic Nursing Board Diploma (OND) on 23rd July.

During that last month, I was not sure what lay ahead. Should I stay on as a staff nurse to consolidate my training? I decided that was not something I wanted to do. Should I return to Orsett? That was an option and with the return, I would inevitably be seconded to the two year Diploma in Nursing course. Having enjoyed my independence, did I move away and seek employment elsewhere? But the Diploma was something I really wanted to achieve and it was available at Orsett. Eventually I decided to return, so I made an appointment with Miss O'Neill and requested a staff nurse post at Orsett, with the opportunity to undertake the Diploma in Nursing.

Although Miss O'Neill was happy to take me back, she informed me the post was on night duty. I was not happy with this and said so; however, her mind was made up: either I accepted the post or I was not going to be employed there. I did accept but requested to work in Accident & Emergency. Miss O'Neill agreed and although it was not clear to me at the time, she was helping me develop my career. In the 1970s, promotion to sister/charge nurse was much more likely on night duty than on day duty and clearly, this was her intent. Looking back, I well remember her words: "You will go on nights and sink or swim. I expect you to swim!"

6 MINORS' AND MAJORS'

At midnight on Friday 5th September 1975, seven people were injured in a crash involving a car and an articulated lorry on the A13 near Grays. The car was coming from the Circus Tavern (a local nightclub) to Orsett Hospital. It was split in two with the engine and front wheels separated from the rest of the vehicle, the left-hand side was ripped off and the bonnet thrown some 40 feet away. Inside the car were four student nurses from the hospital and two of their boyfriends. The lorry driver made the seventh casualty.

When Judy (my staff nurse colleague) and I received the emergency call from ambulance control, we immediately informed the night sister, A&E doctor, radiographer and the on-call surgical team. As the casualties arrived, Judy quickly assessed their condition. One of the men from the car had suffered head injuries and was wheeled to the accident room. The other man had minor injuries and was sent to the recovery room along with the four nurses, all whom had various injuries including cuts/abrasions, facial injuries and one with possible spinal damage. The lorry driver was suffering from minor injuries.

Judy and the surgical team stayed in the accident room with the man who had head injuries while the night sister, a nurse from the wards, the A&E doctor and I dealt with the other casualties.

All required an X-ray so an additional radiographer had been called in from home. Because so many patients' wounds required cleaning/dressing or stitches we decided to create a priority list for X-ray and to get on with dealing with the wounds. At one point in the early hours we decided to put Anglepoise lamps along the corridor from A&E to X-ray, line the casualties up and dress the wounds as they moved along the line like a conveyer belt, something that could never have happened during the day.

By 6am three patients had been admitted and four discharged. By the time the day staff arrived at 8am the department was empty and we were asked if we had had a quiet night! For me, it was my first experience of a multi-casualty incident and I have to confess I really enjoyed the adrenaline rush.

I started back at Orsett in August 1975. I had left Moorfields, been on holiday, and had applied and been accepted for the Diploma in Nursing course starting in September at Basildon College. Salaries had improved and with my night duty allowance, my net pay was £2,440 per annum.

On my return to Orsett, I could see how well the new build had progressed and the ward block, kitchens, and dining room were nearing completion. The new mortuary was now the public and hospital mortuary and the old public building in Grays closed.

The temporary dining room was still in the new workshop building and with its Formica tables and plastic chairs, it was very different to the old dining room and its laid tables and white linen tablecloths. The doctors and sisters/charge nurses were now using the same dining area (much to the displeasure of the consultants) and although self-service had replaced waitress service for the majority of staff some years earlier, now the consultants and senior nursing staff had to queue with a tray in hand. The traditions for staff were changing fast and much more was to come.

The A&E Department was set out in the same way as I remembered from my student days: on two sides ('minors' and 'majors') with a central waiting room. The large plant in the waiting room had gone and some of the leather chairs replaced with more conventional waiting room seats. Patient registration was by hand with biographical details and a brief indication of the problem recorded on both the casualty card and in the very large desk register.

Any patient who walked into the department was registered and unless they looked 'unwell' or were complaining of chest pain, abdominal pain or bleeding, they were routinely sent to the waiting room. Waiting room patients were not normally seen by the nursing staff until called in to see the doctor.

The minor injury side of the department had four trolley bays, a room used for both eye examination/treatment and wound suturing and an examination room linked to the doctor's consultation room. The patient was called from the waiting room into the consultation room, the doctor would examine them then the nurse would carry out treatments in the minors' area.

The majors' area comprised a one-bed resuscitation room (known as the accident room), three single rooms and a large room with a cardiac bed and four trolley bays (commonly known as the recovery room). A full size operating theatre and an anaesthetic room were located next to the large room. Staff offices and restroom were also located on this side of the department.

Unlike emergency departments today, the department had relatively little equipment and no computers. There were two anaesthetic machines, one in the plaster room routinely used to anaesthetise patients who required manipulation of a fractured bone and one in the theatre. Packs for emergency childbirth, opening a patient's chest for internal heart massage and an amputation pack were stored on shelves in the accident room. There was a range of leg and arm splints and various surgical packs and wound dressings. There was also a cyanide antidote box though I am sure the patient would have been dead before they got to us. Although some intravenous fluids such as saline, saline with added glucose and other similar solutions came in plastic bottles or collapsible bags, many others were still manufactured in glass bottles. We also held bottles of artificial plasma. Syringe drivers did not become available until the 1980s and although IV pumps were beginning to be used on the wards there were none in A&E. There were a range of drugs but very limited compared with today.

The normal complement of A&E staff for night duty was two staff nurses. If the department was extremely busy or seriously ill/injured patients were arriving, the hospital night sisters would help during these times. Some nights, and commonly at six in the mornings if the wards had staffing difficulties, one of the two staff nurses was sent to the ward leaving just the one staff nurse in A&E. Although Friday and Saturday nights could be busy, well into the early hours, most weeknights the department was empty by 12.30am.

Nurses still worked a 40-hour week. The night shifts were 12 hours in length, starting at 8pm and finishing at 8am. Full-time staff like me worked four nights one week and three the next. Although this was my roster when the college was closed, when undertaking study days at the college it was classed as a working night, so I worked three nights a week. As college was on a Tuesday, I could guarantee Monday and Tuesday nights off and this meant I worked many Friday, Saturday and Sunday nights. I have to say I enjoyed this as Friday and Saturday were the busiest nights and for me, that meant more experience of a whole range of patients and conditions.

For my first two or three nights I worked with two staff nurses, which gave me a chance to settle in before I would become one of just two staff nurses. Although I had worked in A&E as a student this was very different. On duty, apart from the two staff nurses, there was one doctor at senior house officer level (often quite junior), a porter and the radiographer along the corridor in X-ray. I had started mid-week so although the department was reasonably busy during the hours leading up to midnight, throughout the early hours only a trickle of patients attended. The hospital dining room had a night cook who provided a full menu of hot food until 2am. Many of the hospital night staff regularly used the dining room for dinner but with A&E, I would often go and bring back a full roast or fish and chips to the department.

During the early hours of the morning, local police officers would drive up to the department and both officers would have a break and a cup of tea with us. Although Mrs Stephen the night nursing officer disapproved, I could see the benefit of keeping a good relationship with the on-duty police. On more than one occasion when we had problems, they would arrive rapidly and deal with the situation.

Such a close working relationship sometimes brought problems around confidentiality. When a crime had been committed, the police would often ask us to speculate as to whether a patient had injuries consistent with the crime. Usually we were non-committal but one night when I had been working there for several weeks I was asked if I had treated any wounds that could have been caused by broken glass. It was 3am and I had only seen one person in the last hour with an injury consistent with glass, so I decided to provide that person's name and address. I discovered later that he was indeed the intruder who had broken into a GP surgery and was now in police custody.

The second week I was one of the two staff nurses on duty and realised what a very large learning curve I had to scale, and in a very short period of time. Both sides of the department were kept open until all the patients had left. This meant that one staff nurse would be on majors/admissions and the other on minor injuries. When a patient was ready for transfer to the ward the nurse on the minor side had to look after the patients on both sides until the other staff nurse returned.

If a patient had hospital notes, we were expected to go to medical records and find them. The medical records department was directly opposite the A&E corridor and all notes were stored upstairs. Having put on lights and entered the notes area, it was a different world. Shelves from floor to ceiling crammed full of folders, there were also piles of notes on the floor and the space between each shelving unit meant I had to walk sideways to get between one shelf and the next. If the small windows at ceiling level had been left opened I often disturbed the birds that had settled for the night. If I was lucky the notes were filed in the correct alphabetical order but if not it was a case of a temporary set of notes until records staff could trace the originals the next day.

When we arrived on duty at 8pm the waiting room was often still quite busy with a number of patients suffering from minor injuries such as wounds, sprained ankles, bumps, and bruises. Some of the trolley patients on the minor side would have lower leg fractures, dislocated shoulders or minor illnesses. On majors would be a number of patients ranging from people with abdominal pain, chest pain, gynaecological conditions as well as acute breathing difficulties. Some of these patients would have been referred directly to on-call surgical or medical teams from the GP. Others would need to be seen by the A&E senior house officer and then either treated and discharged or treated and referred.

Although many of the part-time staff nurses I worked with were competent, I very quickly realised that Judy and Kathy were the two staff I relied on most to teach me emergency nursing skills. Over the next few weeks, they explained how to pass the lavage tube into the stomach of a patient who had taken a drugs overdose. This required me to assess the patient's consciousness, instruct them to open their mouth and then pass a very large bore tube down the throat, giving instruction to swallow and keep swallowing. Once the tube reached the stomach, some stomach contents usually emerged into the bucket. A funnel was attached to the tube and with warm water, the lavage commenced. Once the water coming back was clear of tablets, the tube was removed. On some occasions, several litres of water was required before the lavage worked.

I was taught how to stitch wounds. This was initially with silk suture material in people with scalp wounds. Many of the patients had reasonable amounts of alcohol on board so did not feel the needle and because the hair would cover the scar, it was the best part of the anatomy for me, as a novice, on which to practise. I was shown how to apply plaster of Paris casts, advised how to support bereaved relatives and quickly learned how to deal with drunk and aggressive patients. I have to confess my application of plaster of Paris was not the best and did not improve over time. That well shaped, smooth plaster cast that was supposed to emerge did not happen. I am sure many of my casts were replaced after the first visit to the fracture clinic.

One of the procedures I had seen performed when a student, but now had to undertake myself, was to trephine a finger or thumbnail. Many people, especially amateur DIY enthusiasts, hit their finger or thumb with a hammer. Bleeding occurs under the nail and it is excruciatingly painful. To relieve the pressure I would light a methylated spirit burner, heat a straightened paper clip until it was red hot then, with one quick move, apply the hot end to the nail. Almost instantly, the heat would burn through the nail and blood would come gushing out of the hole, with instant relief for the patient. A small dressing was applied to allow drainage to continue and the nail would heal within a few days.

Although this 'see and do' method of training is now frowned upon, it enabled me to become a full member of the team very quickly and with the diploma course and my natural need to link knowledge with actual practice, for me doing and understanding quickly came together.

Every evening as soon as I was on duty, I ensured all the key equipment was working correctly. I checked the suction equipment, oxygen delivery, and the defibrillator. The monitor/defibrillator was a huge red machine that stood about four feet five inches from the floor and although on four wheels, it was extremely heavy to push. Known as 'the red devil,' this machine stood next to what we called the cardiac bed. All patients suspected of suffering a heart attack were nursed on this bed and attached to the monitor. When ready for admission to the ward, the patient would be transferred on the bed and a replacement bed brought back to the department. As there was only one 'red devil' in the department, when more than one person was suffering from chest pain it was a case of deciding who appeared to be in most need of being monitored.

The machine that we used to record a 12 lead ECG was, by today's standards, ancient. It was comprised of wires attached to four small metal plates that, when covered in electrode jelly, were attached to the patient's limbs. A wire attached to a suction cup allowed readings from the chest. By moving the suction cup to each position, further readings were obtained. To record the ECG I had to switch the machine to each separate recording 12 times.

* * *

By mid-September, I had started my Diploma in Nursing course at Basildon College. Numbers on the course were low and included colleagues from various wards and departments from both Orsett and Basildon hospitals. A tutor from the School of Nursing, Margaret Curran, was also one of the students. The first year of the Diploma focussed on health, social change and human physiology, while the second year covered generic illness and a chosen speciality. To continue to the second year, I had to be successful in the first year examinations.

For me, working nights was ideal study time. The department was normally empty by 1am and even on a Friday and Saturday it was clear by 3am. As most of my colleagues had young families, and the idea of going home to sleep was not an option, they would often have a few hours' sleep in the staff room. That gave me the chance to sit at the reception desk and study. When the occasional patient arrived I would call the doctor from his bed (the doctors had a night room in the department) and once the patient was treated and either discharged or admitted to a ward I would return to my books.

During the autumn of 1975, UK junior hospital doctors were starting industrial action over new contracts that would reduce their income. Although there was no disruption of services at Orsett some minor disruption was occurring at Basildon.

The industrial dispute rapidly gained momentum and by Monday 27th October, junior doctors were working to rule in all hospitals (including Orsett), and only emergency patients were being admitted. This continued throughout November and by the end of the month both Orsett and Basildon hospitals had many services closed. The medical consultants decided the only way to maintain a safe emergency service was to close Orsett Hospital entirely. At midnight on Sunday 31st November the A&E department was closed and over the next few days, all ward patients were transferred to Basildon. Basildon continued to only admit emergency patients.

All nursing staff were transferred to Basildon where the A&E department was larger than the one at Orsett. It had two very large resuscitation rooms, a large trolley area, and two single rooms. The closure of Orsett continued throughout the Christmas period and because the college was closed, I was back working full time. Nights were busy throughout the week and extremely busy at weekends. There was no chance of me studying during this period. Christmas Eve was very busy with many casualties suffering injuries as a result of alcohol. One man who climbed off the trolley with a full urinal in his hand, very unstable because of alcohol, suddenly lost his balance. Although I moved very quickly I still received a slight showering, but fortunately most of the urine ended up on the floor with the patient lying in the lake laughing and swearing.

That Christmas Eve was also my first experience of emergency childbirth. I was called outside to help a young girl who was extremely distressed saying that she had "terrible belly pains." I helped her into a wheelchair and took her to a cubicle. While I was trying to take her history, my colleague Judy intervened and asked if she was pregnant? The answer was an emphatic "No." As Judy was far more experienced than me and had an eye for such situations she quickly examined the girl and told her she was pregnant and in labour. I rang the midwifery unit and asked for a midwife to come straight over to A&E. I collected the emergency childbirth pack from the main A&E store and on returning to the room witnessed the birth. The young girl was screaming with pain and genuinely did not seem to appreciate what was happening. The baby's head emerged followed by the rest of his body, a healthy boy. Even with the baby born, the girl continued to deny she had had sexual intercourse and it left Judy to discuss what was to be done with the parents and the girl. Later that night, Judy, in her normal forthright way, said to me: "How the hell did she think it happened? It might be Christmas but she's not the Virgin Mary!"

When we had a lull, I would stand by the ambulance doors and look across to the large Christmas tree outside the main entrance. Festooned with coloured lights, the branches of the tree swayed in the breeze and all seemed well with the world.

Although the doctors' dispute officially ended on Christmas Eve, it was not until after Christmas that patients started to return to

Orsett. Many of us were convinced that the management would use the closure of the A&E as an opportunity to shut it permanently. However, our fears were not borne out and on New Year's Eve the department reopened. As the majority of the public were unaware of this it was the quietest New Year's Eve ever. At midnight, with no patients in the department, Judy, the porter, radiographer, doctor and I celebrated the arrival of 1976.

As the new year began, so patients started to return and it was not long before the department was back to normal. I continued to nurse a whole range of patients many of whom became regular visitors. There are a small group of people whose lives appear to be far more complicated than others. They face challenges both due to the socio-economic conditions in which they live, their mental or physical health and for many their lack of ability to connect with mainstream society. These were our 'regulars' and although I had only worked in the department for five months I had met them all several times.

Although some could be difficult, the majority were polite and often apologetic for not being able to cope with life. We were seen as the lifeline that they held on to in the early hours of the morning when there was no one else. Many of those who were drunk were nursed on mattresses on the floor of the single rooms. This kept them safe from falling from the trolley. It was a new experience for me providing care while kneeling on the floor of the treatment room.

Steve regularly cut his wrists, took overdoses of paracetamol and then arrived by ambulance, often having dialled 999 himself. He was a regular user of the psychiatric services and although he had a partner and young child he was a very dysfunctional chap. Routinely we would wash out his stomach, suture his wounds and refer him to the on-call psychiatrists, only to see him back in the department the following week in a similar state. One evening I was suturing the same wounds that I had only stitched two nights before when he suddenly threw himself off the trolley. I stood there holding the suture needle and thread still attached to his wrist. I told him I had no intention of getting down on my knees to complete the job and he should get himself back on the trolley. Complying with my firm request, the suturing was completed. I wished him goodbye with the words "see you soon".

Jenny was a similar case who regularly came in having taken an overdose of paracetamol. She was so used to swallowing the stomach lavage tube, I would ask her to open her mouth, introduce the tube, and before I had a chance to give instructions, she had swallowed the tube and was holding it in place ready for me to attach the funnel and introduce the water. One of the many nights I was working alone, I had put the tube down into her stomach, filled the funnel and was starting the lavage when a patient in the next room collapsed. I told Jenny to hold onto the tube and funnel so I could rush out to deal with the collapsed patient. When I returned she had refilled the funnel several times and performed her own stomach lavage.

Working alone was never easy and of course not always safe. As the sole staff nurse on duty, I would move from minors to majors whenever needed. It was often a case of going over to minors and dressing a wound, straight back to majors to assess an ambulance admission, and then back to minors again to perform some other duty. Any takeaway medication (TTA's) prescribed by the doctor was also in my remit to dispense. While some drugs came in handy, take-away size bottles, more often it was a case of counting out a given number of tablets from a large bottle and putting them into an envelope. I would write the name of the tablets on the envelope with instructions as to when to take them. Then at 10pm when the receptionist left I had to cover the reception desk.

One night when I was on my own the department was very busy. At 9pm ambulance control informed me there was a bomb alert in the Dartford Tunnel (linking Kent with Essex under the Thames). I rang the night sister and told her. Her response was: "Not to worry dear. I'll send you some help". I was expecting, at least, my staff nurse colleague (who had been sent to help on the wards) to be returned. Instead, a third-year student nurse arrived. Just before 10pm ambulance control sent a message for us to stand down. I said to the receptionist "you can tell them we haven't even stood up!" A more immediate response was forthcoming when a cruise liner returning to Tilbury cruise terminal had hit a storm in the Bay of Biscay, this caused several passengers to be thrown around the ship and sustain injuries, some with fractured limbs.

Working in A&E gives you a real insight into local society. You know the good as well as the problem pubs and clubs, and the people you would not like to meet outside of the department. You know the good areas to live and the areas best avoided.

A&E departments are a melting pot of everything good and bad in a community. For us on night duty, it was normally the pubs in Tilbury, and particularly one called the Toot club, where problems occurred. Other hotspots were pubs in West Thurrock and South Ockendon. It was common to have men coming in with battered faces and grazed bruised knuckles. The story was normally "I walked into a door" or "I hit the wall with my fist". I am not sure if they thought we were so naïve to believe the story or if they thought we had never heard that one before.

As Thurrock is only 20 miles from London's East End it meant that some of the local criminal fraternity had links there. In the mid-1970s certain individuals were rumoured to have strong connections with the Krays. Although both Kray twins had been imprisoned in 1969, one particular woman, who I will call Jane, was said to know them. She also ran a criminal network in Thurrock. When Jane arrived in the A&E department two very large, solidly built bodyguards would always accompany her. Knowing her reputation, I would always ensure I put her in a single room rather than one of the curtained cubicles. The two bodyguards would stand outside the door and monitor all comings and goings. It was always a relief when she was discharged.

Interestingly neither Jane, nor others linked to the underworld, ever caused us any problems. Unlike today where violence to health care staff is all too common, then there appeared to be an unwritten code that, as nurses and doctors, we were to be treated with respect. One evening when a patient called Tom arrived, having fallen and broken his leg, I nursed him on a trolley in the minor injuries area. It was yet another night when, apart from the doctor and porter, I was on my own. Tom was a very short thin man in his 70s and had two very tall, burly sons with him. All three were known to be connected to a criminal network.

Being on my own, I was, as usual, rushing between the minors and majors areas. Tom's two sons were full of energy and to 'let off some steam' they decided it would be fun to have wheelchair races across the waiting room, down the corridor to X-ray and back. The porter was scared to approach them and as I passed between both sides of the department, I would ask them to stop. At one point, providing care for Tom, I said: "My life would be much easier if your sons were not causing havoc in the waiting room." Tom immediately asked me to call them into him. As they stood towering above the small frail man I heard him say: "I don't want to hear another word about you causing problems. Get out and sit quietly." With this, they walked out into the waiting room, tails between their legs, and sat down. I had witnessed the family power and respect within that somewhat closed community.

On New Year's Day 1976 a local man called Michael Toomey was murdered. A few nights later one of the most violent, horrible people I have ever had the misfortune to nurse arrived by ambulance. His name was Alf and I had treated him before and I knew he was linked to other very violent individuals in Thurrock. On this occasion, as usual, he was vile and in his drunken abusive way asked me where Michael Toomey was. I said: "In the mortuary." His reply took me aback. "And there'll be another one beside him tomorrow," he growled. I felt a cold shiver travel through my body as it seemed he was threatening me. But as the department was busy, I soon shrugged the comment off. I later mentioned it to the staff nurse working with me and, as Alf had been discharged, I said: "He probably won't remember me anyway."

When I got home in the morning, I switched on the BBC news: "A body has been discovered on Grays beach. Due to suspicious circumstances, the Home Office pathologist has been called in." That same cold shiver returned. I decided to wait until the evening and then, based on further information, make a decision as to whether I should report what I had heard. During the morning, I lay in bed unable to sleep. I walked down to the beach in the afternoon and police were still at the scene. At 6pm the news indicated the death was from natural causes. My relief was overwhelming and I can honestly say from that day to this I do not know what I would have done had it been a murder. If I had reported Alf maybe I would have become body number three? If I had not, could I have lived with the guilt?

* * *

It was in the early hours of the morning and a patient in cardiac arrest was on the way in. As I waited outside the department, through the fog I could see the halo of the blue lights from the ambulance as it headed towards the hospital. The on-call medical staff were down and once the patient was on the cardiac bed we were into full resuscitation. Despite having never dealt with a cardiac arrest in my student or early staff nurse years, I was now well versed in this emergency. In 1976, there were no national guidelines (the Resuscitation Council UK was not formed until 1981 and it took some time before UK-wide guidelines were established) but there was a general process that we all followed. Chest compressions and ventilations were administered and the first drug infused was sodium bicarbonate 8.4%. In addition adrenaline and various other drugs were given and all had to be drawn up and measured. It would be some years before we had prefilled syringes. Defibrillation was used when certain electrical changes occurred in the heart.

After a while, the patient showed signs of a heart output. Still critically ill, the man was in heart block. A temporary pacemaker was required. Normally during such a procedure, the cardiographer would be called in to set up the pacemaker machine (a small electrical box that maintained the heart beat). Delayed due to the fog, although the cardiographer was on her way she had no way of getting in touch (mobile phones were not part of our lives in 1976). It was left up to the medical team and nurses to set the machine running. The medical registrar inserted the catheter wire into the patient's heart; now what settings did we need on the machine? The staff nurse working with me had no idea, nor did the doctors. Trawling my mind back to my days on coronary care (ward 5) I had certain figures in my head that I was sure were the settings of the pacemaker. As I dialled in the numbers, we saw the pacing beat on the monitor linking with the patient's heartbeat. We had been successful and the man was transferred to the intensive care unit.

One Wednesday night when we were resuscitating a male patient, someone from the waiting room ran in saying a lady had collapsed. I left the team and discovered she was in cardiac arrest. I started resuscitation on the waiting room floor, chest compressions followed by mouth-to-mouth ventilations. I asked the patient who had called me to go and inform my staff nurse colleague. Once we got the lady onto a trolley and into the treatment area we continued to resuscitate both patients. Both showed signs of recovery and it was only at this point we discovered the lady was the wife of the male patient. Both were admitted to the coronary care unit and nursed next to each other.

Since I had worked in A&E as a student a new consultant had been appointed. Dr Peter Ernst was one of the new A&E consultants that were taking charge of A&Es across the country. Dr Ernst wanted change, and part of that change was to provide a pre-hospital care system. To say the older generation of sisters/charge nurses was not impressed is an understatement. The protective clothing required to go out to patients at the scene of an incident was reluctantly stored in boxes by the door to the department. When a call came through you had to sort through them to find trousers and jacket that would fit.

My first experience as a team member was a call about a man trapped at the top of a very high industrial chimney. Having put on my protective clothing and accompanied by the SHO, the ambulance took us to the site. As we sped through the streets I felt nervous. It was also the doctor's first such call so we were two novices relying heavily on the experience of the ambulance crew and the emergency teams at the scene.

It was a dark night, cold and windy, and as we got out of the ambulance I saw fire engines, police cars, and other ambulances. One of the ambulance crew pointed towards the chimney. Looking up I could not see the top, yet up there was the patient with ambulance and fire crews. The doctor was reluctant to climb up and I have to say I was not that enthusiastic but realised that this was now part of my job. Fortunately, before I had started my ascent, there was a shout from above: "He's free! We're bringing him down." To my relief, the patient was lowered to the ground and both the doctor and I could provide care in a more secure environment. During my time on night duty, I was to respond to many pre-hospital calls but these were mainly on the roadside and, although challenging, did not require me to become a steeplejack.

* * *

As 1976 progressed, in June I successfully passed Part A of the Diploma in Nursing. The summer was extremely hot and even during the early hours of the morning, the temperatures were well above average. By June/July, sunrise would be around 5am and I would take a chair outside and sit watching the sunrise over the village. It was a wonderful time of day, so quiet and peaceful.

As I became more confident with the treatments prescribed for minor injuries, when someone arrived in the early hours I would often assess and treat the injury. I would write what I had done on a sheet of paper and, before going off duty, post the casualty card and sheet of paper under the door of the sleeping SHO. Although completely against the rules at the time, most of the staff nurses did this as it allowed a doctor who had been working all day, and would work the next day, to get a few hours' sleep.

At 4am one morning, the doctor was up seeing a patient when a man came in complaining of a sore throat. Asked why he felt it necessary to come in the middle of the night, he replied that he wanted to be reassured it was not anything serious. When the doctor examined him, the patient confessed to having a fear of cancer and every time he had even the simplest ailment, he would worry. Although the doctor told him he had a slightly inflamed throat the man pleaded with the casualty officer for a chest X-ray. As the radiographer was up X-raying another patient the casualty officer agreed.

As the man returned with X-ray in hand, I noticed how ill he now looked. His skin colour was pale/grey, he looked very distressed and appeared breathless and in pain. He said: "The pain is back and I feel very weak." On further questioning, I discovered that what he had originally described as 'a sore throat' was, in fact, pain in his throat. This had woken him at 3am and, despite some relief, it had returned, hence his visit. I immediately put the man onto a stretcher trolley and recorded an ECG. The tracing showed the man had suffered a massive 'heart attack'. The on-call medical team were called and the man admitted to the medical/coronary care ward.

Reflecting on the case, it made me realise that although I would still treat a minor injury without medical intervention, there was no way that I would ever dismiss even the most trivial illness without a medical opinion. Had that man come in when the doctor was sleeping would I have sent him home with a simple remedy for his sore throat? If he had come in when we were busy, would the doctor have diagnosed an inflamed throat and discharged him without the X-ray? Of course, the X-ray was totally irrelevant but it did allow the patient to be in the department long enough for his true symptoms to develop.

Although during 1976 I worked most of my time in A&E, the night nursing officer Mrs Stephen had decided I should become familiar with the intensive care unit (ITU). My first night on duty I worked with the night sister who I had met as a student. Sister Gosney remembered me from when we nursed Mr Brown in 1972 and she was aware that I had written the article in Nursing Mirror. One of the patients was having a procedure called peritoneal dialysis which is used when the patient's kidneys have failed. It involved infusing large quantities of fluid into the peritoneal cavity between the chest and pelvis, which enables the body to remove waste normally undertaken by the kidneys. A very large water-filled warming tank was situated at one end of the unit. Here large bags of the fluid lay warming ready for use. Two large bags of fluid would be administered via an infusion set, and then once infused, the taps on the set turned and the fluid would be drained out. Once I had been shown the procedure I continued to nurse this patient throughout the night.

On another occasion, I was with Sister Goram, also an extremely experienced and competent ITU sister. Sister Goram (or Mary-Jo as she preferred me to call her) taught me how to nurse patients on ventilators, deal with intravenous lines, and the importance of continuing essential nursing care such as care of skin, mouth, eyes, and regular turns. The Cape ventilator was a very large machine measuring some four feet high, four feet wide and three feet deep. When patients were connected to the ventilator, drugs to sedate and prevent breathing were used. When the ventilator was in use, excess fluid would build up in the tubes that connected the patient to the ventilator. Each of the large tubes had to be 'milked'. This entailed disconnecting the ventilator and continuing patient ventilation using a resuscitation bag. While one nurse undertook the 'bagging' the other 'milked' the ventilator tubes. Once 'milking' was completed, the ventilator would be turned back on and the tubes would be reconnected to the patient.

When a patient was being prepared to be disconnected from the ventilator the drugs would be reduced to wean them off the machine. Once disconnected it was essential to administer oxygen, monitor breathing and ensure the person was able to breathe normally. The night I was left in charge of the unit a young man (Tony) was being weaned off the ventilator. I had been advised by the day staff to reduce the drugs throughout the night in anticipation of disconnection in the morning. It was my first time in charge, and although I was still new to ITU care, this was the only patient so the enrolled nurse and I felt confident we would be able to cope.

Apart from being connected to a ventilator, Tony was also on skeletal traction for his fractured femur and he had various other injuries. He had two intravenous lines in situ and as the night turned into the early morning, all was fine. I had reduced the drugs and we had regularly carried out all nursing care including 'bagging' and 'milking' the ventilator tubes. At 4am I again disconnected the ventilator and started 'bagging'. Suddenly the young man became very agitated; he was trying to breathe yet was not able to achieve a full breath. 'Bagging' made him more distressed and reconnecting the ventilator made things even worse. By now his skin colour was deteriorating, his lips and earlobes were turning blue and he was appearing to fit. The skeletal traction was swinging from side to side across the bed and the intravenous lines shaking around on the poles. The ventilator was alarming and the dials were going crazy. I tried sedating Tony and increased the dose of the drug to stop him breathing unaided. By this time both the enrolled nurse and I were way out of our depth and I was terrified Tony was going to arrest. I have never been so frightened in my life.

I decided to put out a cardiac arrest call even though it had not happened yet just to get doctors up to the unit quickly. Once the team arrived, and after further sedation, Tony settled, his skin colour improved and the ventilator was back in charge. I was told that the combination of reducing the drugs and the 'bagging' had obviously caused the problem. It was decided to continue with the sedation and reduce it during the day. I was so pleased when 8am came. I had learned a very big lesson that night and one I did not wish to repeat.

* * *

Although I had vaccinated hundreds of patients against tetanus I never thought I would experience nursing someone in ITU with the disease. Taking the report we were told a man was suffering from tetanus and, although not infectious, he needed total quiet, hence he was in a single cubicle. His condition had deteriorated over the last 24 hours and, despite all the treatment, he was not expected to live. I knew tetanus was caught through a wound becoming infected by the tetanus bacteria. Due to muscle spasm, the jaw would become stiff (lockjaw). Other than that, I knew very little about the disease and certainly did not realise how violent total body muscle spasm was until it occurred while I was nursing the man.

I had been told that every movement I made had to be gentle so not to cause the patient any sudden muscle spasm. Although I complied with the instructions, in the early hours of the morning, it did not prevent one massive spasm occurring. Suddenly the man's body went rigid, arms and legs were like steel bars and his neck was in such spasm the top of his head was pulled backwards towards the shoulder blades. His heart rate increased rapidly (as did mine) and he was sweating profusely. I administered a dose of a relaxant drug with little effect and he appeared to be having major difficulty with breathing. Eventually, with the intervention of the medical team, things improved slightly and the muscle spasm diminished. Although no further events occurred that night, sadly the man did succumb to the illness. It was a good reminder to me of the importance of vaccination against such diseases.

7 STEPPING UP AS A CHARGE NURSE

As I drove to work one evening in January 1977, the rain was very heavy and as the night progressed, it turned into a horrendous storm with forked lightning lighting up the sky and extremely loud claps of thunder. Suddenly the hospital's electrical systems failed and although the emergency power kicked in, there were only a few sockets that were linked to the emergency generator. Many of the cardiac monitors and other electrical equipment shut down. At the same time, the power failure set off all the fire alarms throughout the hospital, plus we had essential patient equipment alarming and nurses trying to work in semi-darkness. As we moved quickly around the hospital assessing what was, and what was not, working, I could hear multiple sirens heading our way. Looking out of the window I saw several fire engines heading to the hospital; the fire alarms had triggered an immediate response by local fire crews. As several firemen entered the hospital with axes poised I was sent to meet them and liaise until we were sure the hospital was safe.

This was just one of the new responsibilities I faced since my appointment as charge nurse on night duty the previous September. I do not recall an interview but that was not unusual at Orsett, especially if Miss O'Neill had decided you were ready for promotion. My uniform was now a white coat (the same as a doctor) with a dark blue embroidered label 'charge nurse' above the left pen pocket. This coat meant I had to now wear a collar and tie, something I became quite used to despite it being impractical for the clinical setting. As part of my promotion, I joined other junior sisters/charge nurses on a first line management course.

As I was still undertaking my Diploma in Nursing I was again having Monday and Tuesday nights off, so as before, most of my nights on duty were towards the end of the week and weekends. Getting into the second year of the diploma was quite a challenge. Although I had been successful in the first year exams, because only two of us were successful, Basildon College decided not to run the second year. Margaret Curran (the other successful student) and I frantically started contacting other colleges to see if we could join their second-year class. I had written to the London Hospital School of Nursing. The tutor to the diploma course was sympathetic to our plight and decided, despite her class being full, that we could join it. As the course was held in the evening, every week Margaret and I drove up to the East End, spent the late afternoon in the school's library, then went to our evening classes. It really did us a favour because the high calibre of lecturers at the London, from both nursing and medical staff, would never have been achieved at Basildon.

Having been both a student and staff nurse at Orsett, I was very hesitant the first night I was working with the nursing officer (Mrs Stephen) and the sisters who, until that night, had all been my superiors. Of course, Mrs Stephen was still my boss but I was now equal with the sisters (not in experience but at least in rank). I need not have worried, as they were all very welcoming. Mrs Stephen, in her usual way, set out the rules that I was to follow. I would be in charge of a number of wards and would liaise with the ward staff, undertake ward rounds and make decisions on when or if to call the doctor. I was to undertake the medicine round on any of 'my' wards that did not have a staff nurse (often most of them did not) and I was to ensure all wards were settled and lights out by 10.30pm. Mrs Stephen expected all the night sisters and me to be back in the office by 10.30pm.

Most nights there was Mrs Stephen or a senior sister in charge plus two sisters/charge nurse on duty. When we arrived at 8pm the day nursing officer would report on the patients from each ward and point out any of particular concern. Each ward had a summary book listing every patient by name, age, and diagnosis. Various columns would indicate specific events such as admission date, date of surgery (if applicable) and a dependency rating. The scale ranged from a dependency rating of 4, indicating the person was 'up and about' and almost ready for discharge to the rating 1a which indicated the patient was critically or terminally ill. By listening to the report and checking the dependency levels across the whole ward, it was easy to identify how busy the nurses were likely to be in any given ward.

Once the report was finished, I would be allocated my wards. The hospital was divided in half with one of us taking wards 3, 5 and 6 and the other sister/charge nurse taking wards 7, 8, 9 and 10. ITU (ward 4) was staffed by registered nurses, as was A&E. The nursing officer or senior sister would have overarching responsibility for the whole hospital and would start by checking on A&E and ITU. I would always visit the ward I felt was the more dependent first and then work from there. The ward staff had a general routine that they were familiar with. I would speak with the person in charge (usually a second or third-year student) and ensure I visited any patient who was critical or post-operative. Once I had given out the late medicines, I would move on to the other wards. Apart from the usual medicines, it was common to dispense prescribed alcohol such as sherry, brandy or even Guinness. A patient who was terminally ill would be prescribed 'Brompton mixture,' a mix of morphine, alcohol and other substances. All patients who received a small tot of alcohol, a glass of Guinness or the Brompton mixture often slept well! As a charge nurse, I had a bleep so staff on any of my wards could contact me throughout the night.

Unless anything untoward happened, the wards were normally settled by 10.30pm and lights out. It was expected that staff kept the ward quiet during the night and telephones were set to mute with a flashing light indicating when a call was coming in. As the bedpans were made of stainless steel it was essential that care was taken when emptying and sterilizing them in the sluice as they could make quite a racket.

One of the less enviable tasks for us when returning to the office was to complete a midnight return. One of us would have to go through all the ward summaries and list on the empty midnight return sheet any admission or discharge in the last 24 hours, thus giving an exact number of patients at midnight. None of us enjoyed this task and as it was always the first person arriving back that was allocated, we always tried not to be first.

Two porters (one in A&E and one general porter), one switchboard operator, a radiographer and the nursing and medical staff made up the staff complement at night. The night sisters/charge nurses took full responsibility for the hospital site. If there was a problem in the nurses' homes, we had to go and investigate. Although we no longer locked the doors to the nurses home (that stopped when the age of consent went from 21 to 18years of age), if any excessive noise or rowdy parties with gate-crashers occurred we were expected to sort it out. The bleep would go off and Pearl from switchboard would say: "Charge nurse, there's a fight in block 12. I've called the police." I would go over to see who was involved and it normally was one of the student's boyfriends attacking a rival. Once all was calm, I would then have to reprimand the student for having men in the block. Usually, the threat of dismissal from the hospital quickly had the student telling the boyfriend off and sending him on his way.

It is funny to recall how the hospital and grounds were so open. Doors to the hospital were not locked and I would happily stroll the grounds at night, while walking the corridors of the hospital never worried me at all. Once a year we would have an anti-abortion group leave a wreath outside the outpatients department after they held a candlelight service. After that was over one of us would go out and bring it inside so it did not cause distress to patients the next morning.

We had a routine. Following supper, we would start the rounds. Like the sisters and charge nurses before me, I would walk into the quiet semi-dark ward and with one of the nurses, I would take the torch and move from patient to patient. As I had been asked in the past, so I would ask the student about the patient and what they understood about the condition. Once complete I would move on to my other wards.

I always enjoyed teaching during the early hours. As most wards were staffed by students, it was a great opportunity for them to learn more about the various conditions and relate these to the patients they were nursing. So much so that I recommended to the newly appointed director of nurse education that a clinical teacher post should be established on nights. It is a position I would have applied for. He was not interested, yet many years later when we met at a national nursing function he admitted to me that he wished he had taken my suggestion more seriously and established such a post.

Although my main responsibilities were now the wards I still had the opportunity to help in both A&E and ITU. Christmas Eve was very busy in A&E so I was asked to go and help. Numerous patients had minor injuries, a number were drunk but happy and the stretcher area was busy with patients needing admission. Several road crashes had occurred ending the year with the A13's toll of 17 killed and 885 injured. It was not surprising the local paper called the A13 "the killer road" and it was going to be many more years before the new A13 would be built.

* * *

On Christmas Eve just after midnight, an ambulance arrived with an elderly lady who had collapsed and died in the street. It was common practice in those days for the ambulance crew to bring the person to us for certification of death and then they would convey the individual to the mortuary. As the SHO went into the ambulance to certify death, I took the husband and daughter to the office. Once I had confirmation, I told the two that the lady was dead.

The husband looked ashen and said very little. The daughter said that her mum had left her house having had a nice evening with the family. She told me how, due to the mild weather, her mum decided to walk home, and as she was about to turn the corner they both waved to each other. As the daughter went back indoors she was looking forward to her parents coming to Christmas lunch the next day. It appeared that the lady had only just turned the corner when she collapsed and had what is known as a sudden death. Although over the past year I had told many relatives that their loved ones had died, that night is still very fresh in my memory, probably because of the circumstances and the time of year. While most people in the area were celebrating Christmas, for this family Christmas Day was always going to be tinged with sadness.

I am often asked how I handled telling relatives about a sudden death. It's never easy but I was always open and honest. I gave the relatives time and space and accepted any reaction from tears or anger to screaming or silence. In my early days, I watched doctors and nurses carrying out the task and some were great while others were hopeless. In A&E, some of the SHOs were very poor communicators and if I were working with one of them, I would ensure I got in first and told the relatives. Often that stopped the doctors getting involved and making a bad situation even worse.

My own father's death in 1997 was sudden. Bereaved relatives had often told me that they could remember every detail of such a day and, from my experience, I now know this to be true. Friday 18th April 1997 started like any other day. Dad left the house and his parting words were "Don't forget to do your lottery numbers. See you tonight." He never came home as he had a cardiac arrest at work and died. A few weeks earlier, Dad, being a carpenter, had restored a pair of church gates and made a new notice board. The vicar at a Rogation Day service rededicated the gates in memory of Dad.

For health care staff undoubtedly the most difficult cases are when telling relatives their loved-one may have committed suicide. On one occasion a call from ambulance control alerted us to the imminent arrival of a man who had hung himself. He was in cardiac arrest and I could see a large mark around his neck. He had tied a rope, suspended it from the garage rafters (a common place for suicide) and having stepped from the chair was found dangling. Due to the internal neck injury, the anaesthetist found it impossible to place a tube into the trachea for ventilation. An emergency tracheostomy was performed but resuscitation was unsuccessful.

These cases are always very difficult to handle as I discovered on another Sunday evening. Dave was dragged into the department by his mates. He had taken an overdose and refused any treatment. Despite me explaining it was essential that I either 'washed his stomach out' or gave him medicine to make him sick, he was having none of it. Following an assessment by a psychiatrist and a mental health social worker, he was considered to be competent and not suffering any mental illness. Despite all of us trying, again and again, to persuade him to accept treatment, he sat on the stretcher trolley and told me exactly what I could do with the stomach tube. He walked out of the department, with his mates still shouting at him to have treatment. I never saw him again.

On the 17th January 1977 a local ambulance was involved in a road crash. I knew both crew members from my nights in A&E and I was devastated to hear Tony had died. The other crew member, Kevin, had sustained leg injuries and was on ward 3. The night before his colleague's funeral I was in charge of the ward. During the medicine round I tried to encourage Kevin to take a sleeping tablet so he could have a reasonable rest before the funeral the next day. He declined but then during the early hours, and having had no sleep, he asked for a sleeping tablet. As the guidelines said not to administer those tablets after midnight, I refused his request. By the morning Kevin was very agitated and the day staff organised some sedation to help him through the funeral. During the service I saw Kevin looking so distressed I realised then that I should have ignored the guidelines and given him a sleeping tablet. I vowed from that day that I would use my own judgement on such matters and not follow some arbitrary guidelines that probably had no sound basis in practice.

As a night charge nurse, I was now becoming much more confident in my own judgement and if a patient was unwell during the night I would recommend a whole range of observations and interventions before involving the doctor. On many occasions, the intervention meant I didn't need to call the doctor and the patient improved. One frustration was when an intravenous line would stop working. Nurses in those days did not insert cannulas, mainly because of rules that had been imposed by the 'extended role of the nurse' document. So it was always a case of getting the doctor out of bed. Thank goodness thinking has changed and now nurses regularly insert cannulas.

Although as a charge nurse I was not legally allowed to certify death, if a patient who was known to be dying then died in the early hours, it was common practice for the sister or charge nurse to confirm the death. After an hour, and the last offices being performed by the ward staff, the body would be conveyed to the mortuary. In the morning before going off duty, I would ring the doctor and let him or her know they had to visit the mortuary and certify death.

* * *

The new ward block and dining room were almost ready for opening. One night, three of us decided to have a sneak preview of the new wards. We thought the easiest way was to get into the goods lift between the kitchen and dining room then proceed from there to the ward block. What we had not realised until we were in the lift was there was no way to open the doors from the inside. We were trapped and sister Cummings declared: "Well, that's our careers over. Here we are, the three people in charge of the hospital, trapped in a lift we shouldn't be in!" Fortunately, as we banged and shouted, George the night porter came into the kitchen. After he had let us out we swore him to silence and no one ever found out (until now) about that night.

STEPPING UP AS A CHARGE NURSE

By March 1977 although I was really enjoying my night charge nurse role, I knew my heart was in A&E. It was possible to get a charge nurse position in A&E without an A&E qualification, but I knew I stood a better chance if I had one. Having investigated, I applied for the course run at the Radcliffe Infirmary Oxford. I knew I would not be seconded, as the only course any nurses were sent on by the hospital was for ITU. I was offered an interview in June which was a particularly busy month for me as I was revising for my diploma exams, our street was planning a Queen's Silver Jubilee street party and now I had to prepare for an interview.

It did not go well. The Radcliffe tutor did not seem to warm to me at all. I was told I would be notified of the outcome but I knew it would probably be no. And so it was. Now I had to rethink my career. Did I stay at Orsett? Did I move on? I had always had thoughts of nursing at sea either in the Royal Navy or on the cruise liners. I wrote to both but the cruise liners only took nurses with both general registration and midwifery. Male nurses could not undertake midwifery so that career was out. The Royal Navy did employ male nurses on the ships but only at Chief Petty Officer rank. Female nurses were officers so, out of principle, I did not pursue that line of nursing either. Of course, today both options would have been open to me as men can qualify in midwifery and male nurses are officers in the Royal Navy. In fact, in 2015, the most senior nurse in the Royal Navy, the Matron in Chief, was a man.

As the Diploma exams were imminent I decided to hold off from my career search and just concentrate on getting the diploma.

The results were released on 26th August and I had passed. I received a congratulatory letter from Miss Trimble and I knew this would be a major boost for my career.

Having been unsuccessful in my application for the A&E course, and not able to go to sea, I had little time to reflect on 'what next' as events overtook me. One morning mid-week in July 1977, Miss O'Neill told me that, as from Monday morning, I would be the charge nurse of the orthopaedic ward. "But Miss O'Neill, except for night duty I've not worked on ward 3 since I was a student. I've very little experience of orthopaedic nursing" I told her. "No problem," she replied "There are trained staff who know about orthopaedics on the ward. I need someone to manage it." She then explained that there had been a number of problems on the ward. I was aware that both the sister and now the charge nurse had left very suddenly. The rumour was that due to poor patient care Miss O'Neill had intervened. Now she expected me to take charge of the ward and sort out the problems.

After she rang off, I wondered what I had let myself in for. Although I probably had more experience of ward 3 than any other ward, it did have 44 beds and my experience of orthopaedic nursing was extremely limited. While on duty that night I spent quite a bit of time on the ward and started to try to get a feel for what would be expected of me. The following night as I carried out the 10pm drug round I was aware the message had got out. One of the more forthright patients said: "So I hear you're coming to take charge of this ward on Monday? Well, I hope you're going to make a better job of it than the last bloke." He went on to ask: "Will we have to make an appointment to see you then?" I was mystified and asked what he meant. "Well, if we wanted to see the charge nurse he would tell the staff when he would come and see us. He spent most of his day in the office." I immediately reassured the patient that I would see him several times a day when I was on duty and would certainly not be spending my day in the office.

8 JUST ONE CHIEF ON WARD 3

It is fair to say I felt some slight hostility towards me as I entered the ward on that Monday morning. This came mainly from an enrolled nurse and one of the staff nurses who felt the previous charge nurse had been treated poorly. I had not worked with any of the permanent staff though I did know a couple of the staff nurses from when they were students on night duty.

The first morning I made it clear to the staff that I wished them to continue to work as normal while I became familiar with the ward, the patients, and the way the things were currently done. Fortunately having looked after the ward at night, I was familiar with all the patients though not in detail. This enabled me to start with the majority of patients knowing me.

The ward ran in a similar way to how it had during my student days. In the morning, the report was taken from the night staff then the day staff were allocated to one of three areas. The number of qualified staff on duty determined how many areas had an allocated qualified nurse. Students and pupil nurses were allocated across all three areas. There was always one registered nurse in charge (normally the charge nurse or senior staff nurse).

Care of the patients was determined by their individual needs. Some required a bed bath while others could wash themselves. Patients who were fully mobile used the bathroom. Beds were made, observations were undertaken, medicines distributed. Any specific interventions were written in the daily diaries and these were carried out as appropriate (there were two diaries, one morning and one afternoon/evening). Any patients for the theatre were prepared and pre-operative medication administered.

By the end of the first week, I had identified three major challenges that were interlinked and that I had to address as soon as possible. The first was the lack of leadership that had developed on the ward. The second was the confusion surrounding the various diaries. The third was the number of patients that had pressure sores; this was appalling and some were so extensive that large areas of heel or buttock tissue were missing.

In 1977 ward 3 was part of the unit managed by nursing officer Miss Barnard. As the charge nurse, I was clinically in charge of the ward. I managed the staff on a day-day basis and was accountable for all clinical care. I was the 'boss' of the ward and everyone in the hospital, including doctors, physiotherapists, domestic staff and of course nurses, knew it. Unlike today, as a charge nurse I had very little general management to worry about. I had to ensure the nursing roster was made out fortnightly but if any staff were off sick, the nursing officer on duty sorted a replacement. There were no budgetary responsibilities and it was a time when if I wanted a shelf put up I just rang the building department and they came and did it.

Qualified staff numbers per ward were far fewer than today. Most wards had an establishment of one ward sister or charge nurse, two or three staff nurses, the same numbers of enrolled nurses and one or two auxiliaries. The bulk of the ward nursing workforce was student or pupil nurses. Although as a charge nurse I was counted as part of the overall numbers on duty, it was expected that I would oversee and manage the care of all the patients. In addition, a ward clerk undertook most of the general administration freeing me up from much of the paperwork.

Nursing documentation was almost non-existent. Each patient had a Kardex. This held general information about the patient including biographical details, information on certain aspects of nursing care and it was a daily record of any changes or events. In addition, the patient would have an observation/vital signs chart for the recording of temperature, pulse, respirations, blood pressure and weight. Some patients would have additional charts including fluid balance charts or neurological charts.

On most wards, there would be a daily diary. This would include the names of patients who required additional nursing interventions and these would include specific tests, operation day, wound dressings and other such interventions. General nursing care was not recorded as it was 'taken for granted' that this was provided. For example, if a patient was confined to a bed it was normal nursing practice to provide a bed bath, change linen, make the patient comfortable and maintain regular checks.

Other differences included the availability of beds; the ward was very seldom 100% full. The length of a patient stay was longer (many patients in ward 3 were in the ward for weeks or even months) so continuity was maintained. When I returned from two days off, normally very little had changed. Doctors came to the ward at pre-arranged times for the daily 'ward round' and consultants visited once a week. Visiting times for relatives and friends were strictly controlled and short (normally an hour in the afternoon and evenings); we even rang a hand held bell up and down the ward indicating visiting time was over. Although nurses were aware of accountability and autonomy, in reality, nurses did what the sister or charge nurse told them to do.

In meeting the challenges of ward 3, my first major task was to claim leadership. I took all the permanent staff into the office and pointed out my concerns. Following a few dissenting voices I said: "Let me make it clear, there is one chief and you are looking at him." Although not the most appropriate leadership approach, and today probably not politically correct, it worked, and from that day, I had no further issues around who led that ward.

The next step was to address the care issues and in particular, the way the diaries encouraged a lack of care rather than continuity. Initially, I removed the two diary system and introduced the same system in use on other wards. Despite this, I was concerned that care was not good especially around following post-operative instructions. As on ward 9, several consultants treated the same condition but each would have a different set of postoperative rules. For some, the patient would be out of bed on day two while for others it would be day three. It was clear some form of individualised plan was required yet at that time the only thing used on all wards was the Kardex and diary.

I decided to design a simple A4 sheet divided into columns and rows. Each column had a heading such as diet, mobility, hygiene and bladder/bowel. Each day, and if necessary throughout the day, I would indicate the type of nursing care to be provided. The key to the implementaion and monitoring was for me to undertake a ward round every morning. Every patient would be seen, any issues addressed and the care sheet updated. The system was straightforward. The nurses looked at the care sheet and provided the care ordered. There was continuous dialogue between the nurses and me. Throughout my duty span, I walked the ward and everyone knew I was in charge.

Running a ward with a number of consultants, registrars, senior house officers and housemen (junior doctors) was always a challenge, especially when doctors on the same team did not get on and each consultant thought they were the most important person on the ward.

Consultants came on different days of the week, except Mr Kellock, the senior orthopaedic consultant, whose round was at 9am on Wednesdays and Dr Naveratnum, the rheumatologist, who had few patients but insisted his round should also be at 9am on a Wednesday morning. As Mr Kellock was senior, I would always conduct the round with him and the staff nurse would go with Dr Naveratnum (though he would often complain that I should be with him). To settle the matter I suggested he arrive at just after 9am and review all the X-rays before going to the patients. By this time I would be finished with Mr Kellock and then could accompany Dr Naveratnum on his round. He agreed - game, set and match to me.

The most challenging aspect of my role was the need to get the pressure sores healed, prevent other patients developing sores and restore nursing credibility. I had already had a run-in with one of the orthopaedic registrars. He had voiced his concern during a ward round and said it was all due to poor nursing care. While I acknowledged he had a point I was furious that he put all the problems down to us. As I pointed out I had inherited these problems and doctors continuously prodding and poking the wounds often compounded them. "As you blame nurses for the pressure sores perhaps if you leave them to me I will get them healed"? He took me up on my challenge and I thought to myself "what have I done?"

Although there were many patients with superficial sores, the two most challenging cases were one lady's heel and another lady's buttock. The heel wound was very deep, almost to the bone. The buttock wound was horrendous. It was so large I could put my whole hand into the wound and touch the base of the spine. From my experience as a student in the plastic surgery ward, I had learned about Eusol cream and pigskin dressings. I asked the house doctor to prescribe both for the lady with the heel wound. The pharmacy was not impressed due to the cost but the medical staff backed my plan and I started the treatment. I set strict criteria that no one except me was to redress the wound. Although it took several weeks, the wound finally healed. I was so pleased but also annoyed that this wound had occurred in the first place. The lady with the buttock wound was not such a good result. Although the wound was showing some signs of regeneration, the lady was so weak that she died before any real progress was made.

As the weeks went by I was beginning to see real improvements. The permanent staff had settled into the new ways of working and the patient care had improved dramatically. I was now becoming an expert on rigging the traction - and there was a lot of it - from counter traction for those with fractured femurs to skin traction for patients suffering back pain. Pressure sores were healing and with the use of pressure care standards and audit, and the diligence of the staff undertaking regular back rounds (these involved two-hourly turns of patients confined to bed and washing/applying cream to vulnerable skin) no new pressure sores occurred.

Infection was not a major problem on the ward and I am sure this was because I had a dedicated group of domestic staff that regularly scrubbed every nook and cranny. They took pride in the cleanliness of their ward. Another factor was the length of time a bed stayed empty. When a patient was discharged, the bed was thoroughly cleaned and fresh linen applied. The bed would then have time to rest before the next occupant.

Although I was not aware at the time, the ward was being monitored by the senior nursing staff, as was my performance. Clearly the drop in standards under the previous sister and charge nurse was known at district level. Despite my junior status, I had been sent in to turn the ward round. I am not sure if I was chosen because Miss O'Neill thought I could do it or if I was just a quick fix. Whichever it was, it gave my career another boost. After two months, the district nursing officer (Miss Trimble) paid a visit and complimented me on the way the ward had improved. After that, other district officers also visited to see how things were progressing.

Although I was enjoying the challenges of running the ward, by mid-September I heard there was a vacancy for a sister or charge nurse in A&E. Despite some to-ing and fro-ing, including making an application for an A&E post in Yorkshire as a lever to get an interview at Orsett, I was finally offered the position. At last, I was heading for A&E and the career in emergency care that I had dreamed of for so long.

9 RETURN TO A&E

My first day back in A&E on 12th October 1977 saw the department put on 'standby' in case of a major disaster. A fuel train with seven petrol tankers had derailed at Grays station. A large section of the platform had been damaged with concrete, metal, and wood flying into the air. Fortunately, only two people suffered minor injuries and although a large part of Grays was evacuated due to the risk of an explosion, the incident passed without any further injuries.

Arriving in the department on that first morning I immediately felt that I had made the right decision. Sister Hickson was the senior sister and with charge nurse Chandler, Sister Morton and me, this quartet made up the complement of senior staff. On an early shift, there were normally two sisters/charge nurses, a number of staff nurses and students. During the afternoon, similar numbers, and in the evening, usually one sister or charge nurse, plus one staff nurse and four or five students.

Early mornings were very similar to how I remembered them from my student days. They were normally quiet and all staff were engaged in preparing the department for the day ahead. The hierarchical structure was still in place with the staff nurses and students going to coffee in the staff room at 8.30am while coffee for sisters/charge nurses and doctors was at 10.30am. The staff nurses and students made their own coffee in the staff room while ours was brought to our office on a tray from the outpatients' canteen.

Although activity in an A&E department can be unpredictable, it was surprising how structured the day was. Patients often started arriving around 9am. The follow-up clinic (patients needing a return visit for review) would be held in the minor injuries area between 9am-10.30am and after this, all-minor injured patients would use that area. The major side started getting busy around 10.30am or 11am, often with patients seen by their GP and referred to one of the specialist teams such as medicine or surgery.

The consultant (Dr Ernst) would hold a minor surgery clinic two or three mornings a week. Patients with such ailments as in-grown toenails or minor orthopaedic problems would receive minor surgery in the department's operating theatre. Of course, during the day, the routine was often disrupted due to the arrival of an ambulance with a seriously ill or injured patient. When this occurred all appropriate staff would become involved and for patients with minor injuries this meant a much longer wait. The evening shift could be busy or very quiet. As there were routinely just the two qualified staff, one would look after minors and the other majors. Minors had a couple of students and majors, three students.

In November, there was a fire service strike which ran until January 1978. The army was deployed using army fire trucks known as 'Green Goddesses'. Soon after the strike had begun, there was a fire at the Tilbury power station. Troops, part-time firemen (who were not on strike) and police attempted to extinguish the blaze. Due to both lack of equipment and inexperience, the fire raged for two days. Sixteen people (three power station staff and thirteen firefighters) suffered smoke inhalation. Unlike the regular firefighters, the troops and others had very little respiratory equipment so a large number of men arrived in the A&E department after each shift requesting a respiratory assessment. During the first day and night several 'Green Goddesses' would arrive outside the department at regular intervals and 12-24 men would all book in. This continued on the second day and although the fire was then brought under control, it was several days before the troops could leave the scene. To relieve the department, Dr Ernst took himself, a casualty doctor and a nurse down to the power station. As the troops came off shift they were examined and only those that needed a chest X-ray would be sent up to the department.

On a smaller scale there was an incident one morning, across the road from the department, when the tennis court hut went up in flames and the army green goddesses arrived. With thick hoses running across the road in front of the department, we watched with bated breath as a local milk float drove over the ramps of the hosepipe. As the milk crates lurched from side to side, we waited for them all to come crashing onto the road. Fortunately, the milkman crossed the hazard successfully and many of the army firefighters purchased a bottle of milk to quench their thirst. Unfortunately, due to the rather out of date fire equipment, the hut burnt to the ground.

Sister Hickson (I could never bring myself to call her Joan) ran the department in almost military style. This was probably due to her years at sea on the ocean liners Queen Mary and Queen Elizabeth. With her deep voice and marching style walk, I sometimes felt I should stand to attention and salute as she passed. She spent most of her time working on the minor side ensuring that the waiting patients moved through the system at speed. The patients were taken to the doctor in the consulting room (known as the patient to doctor system). Sister would expect the staff to call the next patient into the sub-waiting room and prepare the patient for the doctor. Preparation meant the removal of shoe and sock for any foot or ankle injury, removal of coats/jumpers for arm injuries and for upper leg or chest problems, this would require preparation in the examination room.

Once the doctor had seen the patient and prescribed treatment the nurse would take the individual out into the treatment area and the next patient would be in. Sister Hickson ensured there was no slacking and almost as one patient left, another was installed next to the doctor. On the occasions when the minor injuries area was very busy it was not unknown for sister Hickson to undertake treatments before the doctor had seen the patient and she would simply tell the doctor what she had done so he could record it as his decision. While one might call this the cart before the horse method, no one ever questioned it.

Although the consultant and his deputy (clinical assistant) were available throughout the day Monday to Friday, the majority of patients were seen by the 'casualty officer' or to give the correct title, Senior House Officer A&E. Although this may sound impressive, the majority of doctors were either junior in their years in medicine or had come to England from other countries, some of which had very different cultures and ways of practising than ours. Sister Hickson kept a very strong rein on them. One doctor's writing was so unreadable he was threatened with dismissal. So he arrived on duty with a typewriter, and as he had no idea how to type, the process descended into farce. In the time it took to load the card into the machine and type a few words, a dozen patients could have been seen. The typewriter only lasted one morning.

I learned a great deal from sister Hickson about running an efficient A&E. Lengthy waiting times were not tolerated. Once a decision to admit a patient to a ward was made, she expected the patient to be off to that ward. She discouraged any investigations or treatments that could be performed on the ward.

One morning a patient arrived from the GP with a diagnosis of CVA (stroke) but the medical team were busy on the ward. I went across to minors and explained the situation to sister Hickson. She immediately got the A&E doctor involved and 'encouraged' him to start an IV infusion. The fluid was dextrose/saline. As the fluid entered the patient's vein, he started to recover. The reality was the clinical presentation of CVA was, in fact, a hypoglycaemic event (low blood glucose due to diabetes). With further glucose, within minutes the man had made a full recovery.

A patient with diabetes, especially if insulin-controlled, can suddenly suffer a drop in the glucose level in the blood. This leads to a variety of clinical presentations including aggression, confusion, drunk-like state, or, in this case, mimicking a stroke. In 1977, capillary blood tests for glucose were not available in the department and venous blood tests took time, so the diagnosis was based on history and the sudden onset of symptoms. Clearly, the GP had made a diagnosis without considering the possibility of low blood glucose.

Sunday mornings were normally quiet, shops closed and for many people, Sunday was a day of rest and social activities. As charge nurse Chandler (David) often said: "It's always quiet on a Sunday morning. They get up late, have their breakfast then come to visit." Although he was probably right, I did try to dissuade him from such comments in front of the students. He took no notice and on a Thursday evening he would often declaim: "Gazette night - they won't be in till they've read it." And it was true that Thursday evenings - the day the Thurrock Gazette was published - were often quieter than others. Although David gave the impression of not being happy in his work, he was never a minute late and when a patient needed attention, he was a master at his speciality. Nurses would be hard-pressed to better his wound dressings, bandages, and application of plaster of Paris. Although he was not keen on the majors' side if a trauma case arrived, his care was very slick and his stomach washout was like watching an artist at work.

For some reason all three of my sister/charge nurse colleagues preferred running the minors' side, leaving the staff nurses and me to run majors. To some extent, I could see why they preferred minors, as it was easier to coordinate the department rather than being engrossed in the activities of the majors' area. For me, that meant more time in majors, enabling me to refine my trauma and nursing skills.

As the weeks progressed, I became much more confident in running the department and making decisions on patient care although when a German citizen on a Russian cruise ship was brought in and died I thought there would be challenging complications. Having phoned the coroner's officer I was pleasantly surprised how uncomplicated the incident was. Once we had sufficient details the local police notified the German police to visit the relatives and the coroner's officer took charge of the body and the necessary arrangements.

I enjoyed teaching the students and started giving them short quizzes. This normally required them to do some investigations as many of the questions involved the less routine activities. Over the years, I developed workbooks for the students and newly registered staff, as well as a video for students on how to apply bandages, strapping and dressings.

Common procedures for minor injuries that have now either changed or been discontinued included Elastoplast strapping from toes to the knee for ankle injuries, collodion splints for big toe fractures, thumb spica for sprained thumbs, Vaseline gauze dressings for burns and Robert Jones bandages for knee injuries (several layers of cotton wool and bandages to maintain the leg straight). The cleaning solution for wounds was a very soapy solution called Cetrimide. This, like most cleaning solutions, was in large bottles for multi-use. For wounds with foreign bodies that could not be easily removed, magnesium sulphate paste was applied. Everyone with even the smallest of wounds received a tetanus toxoid vaccination and care in drawing up the dose was required as this came in multi-dose bottles. Potentially infected wounds meant the patient dropping their trousers for an injection of a very large dose of penicillin into their buttock.

My first Christmas as an A&E charge nurse was approaching and I was pleased that I was working Christmas Day and off-duty on Boxing Day. Christmas morning was quiet. The Salvation Army played Christmas carols in the waiting room and we had a very substantial feast laid out in the fracture clinic. The plaster technician had set up his bar in one of the consulting rooms and staff were visiting from all over the hospital.

Suddenly our frivolities were shattered by the arrival of a man with a serious head injury. He was unconscious and following assessment and treatment was to be transferred to the neurosurgical unit at Oldchurch hospital Romford (some 15 miles from Orsett). As both sister Hickson and David Chandler were on duty, it was decided that I should travel with the man to Oldchurch. It was not uncommon for a nurse to go alone with the ambulance crew as very little in the way of portable equipment existed so it was not possible to provide much in the way of intensive care while en route.

The ambulance arrived and off we went. With the police escort in front, we travelled at speed through the streets often in the middle of the road. Suddenly the ambulance veered to the left causing us all to be thrown across the inside of the vehicle. The ambulance driver had not seen the keep left sign in the middle of the road. Although a frightening experience the skill of the ambulance driver prevented a fatal crash.

My main concern was ensuring the patient did not deteriorate further during the journey. The man's airway and breathing were maintained by artificial support. Oxygen was being administered and an intravenous infusion was in one arm. I had to record all vital signs manually. Automated machines to record pulse and blood pressure were some years away as were pulse oximeters. I used my clinical skills of observing the skin colour, skin texture, respiration rate and rhythm and manually feeling pulse rate, rhythm, and volume. Manual blood pressure was impossible in a fast-moving ambulance so clinical observation was essential. Despite the journey, we arrived safely and the man was handed over to the neurosurgeons.

Another transfer on a Saturday afternoon during the spring of 1978 involved me escorting a patient to the Middlesex Hospital in Central London. This again required a police escort and in Central London police motorcycle outriders. We sped through the city streets arriving at the hospital by late afternoon. Once the handover was complete, the two ambulance men and I left. As the crew needed a meal break and I had completed my shift (I was due off duty at 5pm) we decided to take advantage of our unexpected visit to the capital. St Katherine Docks had only been open in its present form since the early 1970s and none of us had been to visit. The ambulance driver parked in the car park and we found a very nice restaurant on the dockside. Having finished our meal we took a stroll around the quay taking in the buzz of this relatively new tourist attraction. Linking work with play was an essential part of emergency care and although this would probably not happen today, it was a great way to de-brief and de-stress.

Apart from transfers by ambulance, we occasionally had a transfer by helicopter. The only helicopters available in the 1970s were either naval or RAF. The landing site was the local cricket ground, just up the road from Orsett Hospital. When a helicopter transfer was to take place, the ambulance would convey the patient from A&E to the helicopter. As we were in a village, the police and fire service would arrive and consequently many spectators would turn up to watch events unfold. One winter the snow was on the field and having loaded the patient, several of us stepped back from the Sea King helicopter as it took off. Unfortunately we did not move back far enough. As the rotor blades spun and the helicopter lifted off the ground a huge snowstorm was whipped up engulfing all of us.

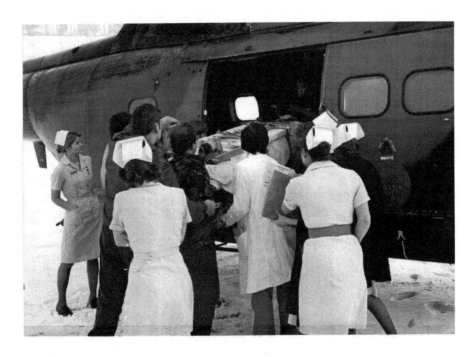

A helicopter transfer in the snow

As Sister Hickson had planned to retire at the end of March, speculation began early in the new year as to who her successor might be. I had decided I would apply but thought that a more experienced external candidate would come forward. However, to everyone's surprise, the advertisement was internal and I knew the only other candidate (if he applied) would be David. I am sure David did not really want the job but the pressure to apply came from Sister Hickson and Sister Morton. In the end we were the only two candidates.

The interview was held on 27th January 1978 and the panel was Mr Gonzalez (divisional nursing officer), Miss O'Neill, and Dr Ernst. I knew all three wanted a modern approach to the A&E. Dr Ernst was looking for someone with a vision for the future and who agreed with his modern approach including the pre-hospital response team.

Although I believed I had shown my commitment to moving the department forward, I was still a relative newcomer to A&E. Despite this, I was offered the post and I am convinced that my success on ward 3 helped me clinch the job. My appointment as senior charge nurse was to commence on 1st April 1978 and my salary would remain the same at £3,539 per annum. Having been appointed it was my ambition to take forward the speciality and, working with Dr Ernst and the nursing staff, make the A&E at Orsett one of the best departments in the country.

On the afternoon of Sister Hickson's retirement party the A&E department was relatively quiet so many well-wishers were able to attend. Formal speeches were given and gifts were presented and then the event became more informal. Around 4pm I was called out of the party by one of the nurses who told me that the two plaster technicians were having a fight in the plaster room. I went in to find both of them shouting and throwing water and plaster rolls at each other. I told them to stop and to calm down. This was not the first time they had rowed but it had never reached this stage. I suggested that as one was due off at 5pm, he should go home immediately and I would pursue the matter with both of them the following week. As I left the plaster room I suddenly realised the responsibility I was taking on, and that was just with the staff!

10 THURROCK'S 4th EMERGENCY SERVICE

The permanent nursing staff included charge nurse David
Chandler, sister Margaret (Maggie) Morton, a number of staff
nurses including Diana Kennedy, Nicki Croften and Mack
Offord, enrolled nurses, two auxiliaries and me as the senior
charge nurse. The nursing workforce also included the student
and pupil nurses who were allocated to the department with each
one spending about six weeks with us. Although I could now
appoint another sister or charge nurse, I decided to hold off from
doing so as Maggie Morton was close to retirement and then I
could appoint Diana and Mack to the two vacant posts. The pair
complemented each other; Mack had many years A&E
experience while Diana brought experience but with a younger
outlook to the service. Both were well liked by other staff
members and would keep the team together.

Having worked several months in the department, I already had
some ideas for change. I knew I wanted to sort two of the main
storerooms and to increase the stretcher trolley capacity on the
minor side by converting the two sitting only bays to stretcher
bays. I also wanted drug cupboards and a proper worktop in the
large room on the majors' side. Using an old stretcher trolley as a
work surface and drugs laid out in wooden boxes was not the
image of a modern department I wished to convey.

I also wanted to integrate the staff more, so instead of a staff
room for staff nurses and students to take their breaks, with the
office for sisters/charge nurses and doctors, I wanted all staff to
use the staff room for breaks and the office to be just that. I'm

not sure if Dr Ernst was impressed but he went along with it. I was determined to maintain the uniform standards, especially the female students, as they had gone from the traditional dress with apron and butterfly cap to a national uniform that, because of its poor quality, was referred to as the 'J cloth dress'. Almost overnight, jewellery and ponytails appeared, something that would never have been tolerated previously and I ensured that trend was short-lived.

Drawing up the duty roster was not an arduous task. Staffing levels in the 1970s were good. I always had enough registered staff and students allocated to the department; this enabled acceptable numbers of staff on duty per shift. Recruitment was never a problem as I had a list of staff who were working in other areas of the hospital waiting to work in A&E.

An early change was making the pre-hospital care clothing and equipment more accessible. Sister Hickson and charge nurse Chandler had never been enthused by this new service. Pre-hospital care provided by doctors (often GPs) or hospital A&E departments was an increasingly popular concept. Even when hospitals did provide such care, the clothing was often inadequate. The nurses and doctors that attended the Moorgate tube disaster in 1975 had gone to the incident in full uniform, nurses wearing dresses, aprons, and large linen caps, the doctors in white coats. At least, our department had protective clothing and boots but it was stored inappropriately and needed sorting.

Looking around the department, the only logical room to adapt for the pre-hospital clothing and equipment was the anaesthetic room. This room, while linked by a door into the operating theatre, was never used other than for storage. It was ideal as it had an entrance directly off the major's side corridor, it was near to the ambulance entrance and enabled the clothing to be hung, boots to be laid out in size order and was a suitable place for staff to change into the pre-hospital clothing.

Once we had cleared and relocated the stored equipment I had the carpenters come up and fit a row of hooks along the length of one wall. With help from the staff, we sorted the clothing and boots into sizes and set them out for easy use. Some of the smaller pre-hospital equipment boxes were also located in the room but the heavier ones were located by the ambulance entrance doors. When everything was in place, I asked the staff to familiarise themselves with the room and, in particular, to practise putting the clothing and boots on so that they knew their size and the time it took to get ready. I was really pleased with the outcome, all the yellow protective trousers and jackets on hangers in size order. David Chandler came over and as he looked into the room he remarked sarcastically: "It looks like a lifeboat station." So from that day on the room was named 'the lifeboat station.' I even had a door sign made and a brass key tag with 'lifeboat station' engraved on it.

Not only was I determined to improve the way the pre-hospital care was organised, and work more closely with Dr Ernst on this aspect of our service, I also wanted the local community to be more aware of it. I invited the Thurrock Gazette to send a reporter along to the department. The local paper had reported on our attendance at incidents in the past. One particularly newsworthy event was on the 6th June 1977 when a car was crushed between two buses in Grays. Two people were trapped in the car which was wedged under a single decker bus for 90 minutes. Despite the efforts of the emergency ambulance crew, and the doctors and nurses of the mobile accident unit, both casualties died. At the inquest in October there was a commendation from the coroner, endorsed by the jury, to the Orsett Hospital Mobile Accident Unit.

The Gazette reporter and photographer came to the department and published an article with pictures. It described our work and how we had attended 12 serious incidents the previous year. It said:

> Badly injured crash victims no longer have to wait to get to the hospital to receive expert medical attention. For Thurrock's fourth and virtually unknown emergency service can be ready to attend any incident in just three minutes.

Another chance to promote the pre-hospital service came at the 999 fair. A part of this annual event was a display of all three emergency services working together at a mock road traffic accident. Peter Ernst and I had a stall at the fair about our service and we were included in the service's display.

I felt it would be good for me to get to know the pre-hospital scene better. With the agreement of the senior ambulance staff, I spent several evenings with the local crews. Thurrock ambulance station had two ambulances running in the evenings and one at night. The ambulance had two stretcher trolleys (one either side

Dealing with a 'car accident' at the 999 fair

Photo: Thurrock Gazette

of the interior) that could also be used to create six seats. Over
the months, I had the opportunity to go to many calls from
domestic incidents to road crashes. The call would come from
ambulance control on a telex machine print-out. Once aboard
the ambulance, the driver would radio in to control to say we
were mobile. I sat in the back on the stretcher trolley, bracing
myself with feet against the second stretcher. Blue lights flashing
and siren blaring we would race through the streets to the
incident. On arrival, the attendant would assess the patient(s) and
he and the driver would provide immediate care while I helped as
requested. Pre-hospital ambulance care had improved over the
years but it still primarily involved first aid with the addition of
oxygen and Entonox (pain relieving gas). Paramedic care was
several years away.

During one summer, I arrived on duty at 8am to be informed that the night sister and casualty officer were out at the scene of a lorry crash where the driver was trapped. They had been there since 6am and they thought it was going to be a lengthy job to cut him free. The lorry had gone through the crash barrier and down an embankment. The cab and engine of the lorry were pushed onto the driver trapping him and causing serious injury. The casualty officer had administered analgesia and established one intravenous line. Oxygen was being administered and the man was in shock.

Having replaced the staff, we were getting reports that the man's condition was deteriorating and he was still firmly trapped so the clinical assistant and I decided to go to the scene. On arrival we had to climb down the steep slippery embankment and into the cab. The clinical assistant decided to perform a 'cut down' into the man's arm to establish a larger intravenous line (this procedure involves the doctor incising into the arm and physically locating a vein). At the same time, further analgesia was given. Once we had two lines with large volumes of fluid going into the man we were ready for the fire service to try again to get him out. It took until 12 noon to release him and, despite his ordeal, thanks to the care provided at the scene, and later in A&E and on the ward, the man survived his injuries.

* * *

It was unusual for the mobile team to be called for a cardiac arrest. Normally the ambulance crew would handle it, starting resuscitation, quickly getting the patient into the ambulance and

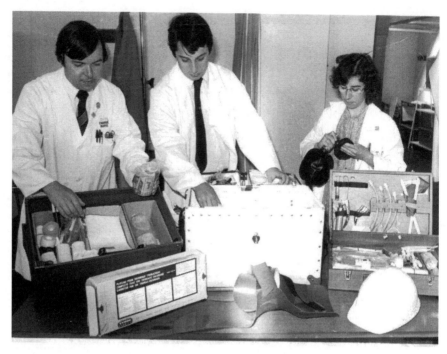

The mobile accident team   *Photo: Thurrock Gazette*

racing as fast as possible to A&E. The difference with this patient
was that, having arrived at the house, the crew found a heartbeat,
yet every time they attempted to move the man, he re-arrested.
When we arrived, I attached him to a cardiac monitor/
defibrillator. When the man was lying still on the bed the
monitor showed a reasonably stable heart rhythm. Yet as soon as
we started to move him his heart went into a fatal rhythm. The
doctor administered drugs designed to stabilise abnormal
rhythms and eventually we were able to transport the patient
back to the department. Once in A&E, the medical team
admitted him to the medical/coronary care unit.

One Saturday evening a call from ambulance control requested
the team attend an incident at one of the large factories along the

Thames to deal with a casualty inside a basement room accessed by narrow external stairs. When we arrived, the doctor and I were informed that the man appeared dead. His throat had been cut and the entrance to the stairwell and stairs were covered in blood. I asked why we had been called if he was already dead. The reply was that the police, ambulance and the company staff were not sure if they should move the man. Also there was some uncertainty as to whether there were any life signs. No one seemed to know if it was an attempted murder or suicide. Although this appeared to be an abuse of our services, we were there so we said we'd try and help.

Going down into the basement with very little light was a challenge. Following the trail of blood, we found the man and it was almost certain that life was extinct. I could not feel any breathing but with the injuries to his neck, it was impossible to assess for any carotid pulse. There was no radial pulse and his heavy clothing made it difficult to feel for a femoral pulse. We needed to get him up and into an ambulance to make a more detailed assessment. Once we got him up there, it was clear that he was dead. It later emerged that he had apparently cut his own throat and then staggered down the stairs and into the basement. The coroner's inquest confirmed suicide.

* * *

The winter's day we were asked to send the mobile team to an incident on the A128 is one I won't forget. A car and van had collided and the car driver was trapped and suffering life-threatening injuries. Peter Ernst drove to the scene in his car and

I was following in an ambulance with other essential equipment. Unfortunately for me the only ambulance immediately available was a non-emergency vehicle with no blue lights or two-tone horns.

As we left the department, snow was falling heavily and the driver, who was not experienced in emergencies, could hardly see through what was now a blizzard. As she drove along the country lanes towards the main road I wondered if we were going to make it. We reached the A128 but, as she accelerated, one minute the ambulance was in the middle of the road, the next it was on the opposite side. With no siren or blue lights, and with a full-blown snowstorm in progress, the driver sounded the vehicle horn and flashed the headlights at oncoming traffic. It was one of the most terrifying journeys I've experienced.

The incident on the A128 is one I will never forget

More by luck than judgement we reached the scene and Peter had already established an IV line. The driver was unconscious and his breathing was very poor. I set out the equipment and assisted Peter as he established a second IV line and administered painkillers. It was difficult to maintain the man's airway through the driver's door, so I climbed into the back of the vehicle to work from there. The Fire Service was cutting the car away from around us but it was taking time and the man was deteriorating. Suddenly he stopped breathing. Peter, now also in the back of the car, was like a circus contortionist, stretching over the man from the back to get a tube down the trachea. Unfortunately, despite all our efforts, the man died.

* * *

On a Sunday morning in May I had a call from ambulance control asking for the mobile team to attend a man impaled on a scaffold pole. Staff nurse Aileen Parsons accompanied the doctor to the scene. On arrival they were met by all three emergency services, and a man in the driver's seat of a car with a scaffold pole going through the front windscreen, piercing his chest and then out of the back of the car. Fortunately the pole had missed most of the vital organs and the man was conscious and talking calmly. Intravenous fluid, oxygen and pain relief was given while the fire service cut the pole at both ends leaving about a foot of it protruding from the front and back of the man's chest.

When he arrived in A&E, the treatment continued and the man sat chatting and joking with staff. Following X-rays and further medical assessment he was transferred to theatre where the pole was removed. Remarkable little internal injuries were found and he made a full recovery. As I was always encouraging the staff to publish, I persuaded Aileen to write up this case history and it appeared in the RCN Emergency Nurse newsletter.

While not a true mobile team call out, on many a dark cold autumn evening we would get a coach driver parking a 50-seater on the road outside the department. The story was usually the same; an elderly passenger had become ill on the way home from an outing. As I got into the coach, I would always be told the casualty was lying along the back row of seats. Once I had assessed the person, rather than calling an ambulance, I would get the porter to align the stretcher trolley below the emergency door and, with help, physically slide the patient through the door and onto the stretcher.

Sometimes going out to a pre-hospital incident can change your perception of the job. One of the staff nurses had handed in her notice and while working her notice, a call came through to the department about a man trapped under a train. It was December 1983 and on arrival at the scene the staff nurse and doctor had to crawl under the train to treat the man. At one point during the rescue the train needed to be moved. The local paper reported what happened next:

> Two of the medical team stayed with the man while the train was rolled backwards. It took a lot of courage.

Exactly what the staff nurse experienced under that train I will never know. She always declined to reveal the discussion she had

had with the man, but on her return, she asked me if she could stay and she withdrew her notice.

Although our mobile care service ran from the hospital it was linked into the Chingford Major Accident Scheme (in later years this became the London branch of BASICS – the British Association of Immediate Care Schemes). Dr Ernst was a member of this group and apart from providing care from the hospital he was also on call from his home in Ilford as I discovered the first time I was invited to his house for dinner.

As I drove there I was feeling somewhat hesitant as I had never had dinner with a consultant before. But as soon as I arrived I felt welcome and comfortable. Peter, as he insisted I called him, introduced me to his wife Margo and to their two young children. Following a very nice dinner, we were chatting in the lounge when the phone rang. It was London Ambulance Service requesting that Peter attend a road traffic accident and so he left immediately. Margo did not really approve of her husband going out at all hours crawling under damaged cars and putting his life at risk. She did, however, recognise the benefit of such a scheme and that Peter was committed to the service (the family car was full of resuscitation equipment and had a green light on the roof). Although it was unfortunate the evening was cut short, from that day on the three of us became great friends and Peter and I went on to work together as partners running the A&E department.

As I had shown so much interest in the pre-hospital service Peter invited me to become a regular attendee at the Chingford doctors' meetings. One evening in the early 1980s, a company rep came to talk about a 'revolution' in communication. He said the doctors could keep in touch with each other at an accident scene by using a 'mobile' phone. He explained that large antennae were being erected across London and one day everyone would be able to carry around one of these new phones. I asked if they could be used outside London and he said it would be possible once the UK network had been established. It all sounded a bit farfetched to me so I suggested to the meeting that they might be buying into something that would prove to be a five-minute wonder. History was to prove how wrong I was! On 1st January 1985 Ernie Wise made the first mobile phone call from St. Katherine Docks in London and within a few years they were in common use.

Apart from the meetings, the Chingford group was often involved in mock major incidents so the emergency services and the doctors could test out their response. I was involved in several of these exercises over the next ten years, either working in the 'emergency department' or at the scene. There was a closed hospital in East London that was ideal for testing the in-hospital aspects of a major incident. Early in the morning, we would set the old A&E up as if it was for real. During the exercise numerous 'patients' (casualty simulation volunteers) would arrive. The doctors and I would triage the casualties and take them through an A&E process. Triage is now commonly used for every patient in all emergency departments in the UK but in the 1970s it was primarily used for disaster situations. One 'casualty' who had been triaged as a category 4, which meant his injuries were fatal, was to be put in a holding area until he died. As I moved him on the trolley he looked up at me and said:

"Please don't let me die. Please don't leave me alone." I felt a great lump come to my throat. Imagine if this was for real. How would I handle such a situation?

Another exercise was to respond to a mock plane crash at Stansted Airport. All airports regularly simulate such events. Having raced up the M11 from Peter's home with sirens and green light flashing, on arrival we were confronted with a plane full of 'passengers' and smoke billowing from the cabin. With the fire service's agreement, we were allowed inside the plane. 'Casualties' were screaming with some getting up from their seats and others trapped in theirs. Luggage from the overhead lockers was strewn all over the floor hampering movement. At one point as I turned, I nearly cut my head on a sharp piece of fuselage which taught me to always wear my protective helmet. As people were moved from the plane to the triage area, I was asked to take charge of their on-going care until they could be moved by ambulance to the hospital. With a number of voluntary first-aiders, we provided a reassessment of care for a whole range of injuries. These opportunities gave me a good insight into major incidents and certainly helped me plan and coordinate the major incident plan for Orsett Hospital.

Apart from an interest in pre-hospital care, Dr Ernst was also very keen to engage with local industry and forge links with other organisations such as police, fire and council staff. This paid off in a whole variety of ways including the opportunity for me to get to know the occupational health nurses from the various industries and to attend the local occupational health nurses forum.

I recall walking across the building site on the foundations of what is now Lakeside shopping centre and discussing potential risks with the occupational health nurse and health and safety manager. We also introduced the first automated defibrillation-training programme for the police in Tilbury Docks. This type of liaison enabled us to be aware of specific hazards. Linking with local industry also benefitted the A&E department, for example Esso donated several pieces of equipment including a blood glucose monitoring machine, portable suction unit, an ECG and portable resuscitation unit. Other companies in Thurrock also contributed essential pieces of equipment.

11 WORK AND PLAY

Apart from the structural changes I was making to the department, I was keen to review the nursing care. Sister Hickson had established a very slick and efficient service but I wanted to set down the nursing practices in written format to ensure all nurses (registered and students) were practising in the same way. I certainly wanted eye-care improved and so I introduced a visual acuity chart and made it clear that every patient with an eye problem should be tested before any intervention. Through my clinical teaching, I also ensured that staff applied eye pads correctly. Incorrect application can risk damage to the cornea as I had learned at Moorfields.

One of the important things for me as a leader was to remain very much a part of the working team. I stayed on the rota and the vast majority of my time would be clinically based. I dealt with a range of injuries and incidents, including a disproportionate number of men stapling themselves to wooden pallets. This stemmed from a local pallet factory which required the men to use high-powered staple guns to connect lengths of wood to make a pallet. Health and safety appeared lax, as we had a steady stream of men arriving with legs or arms stapled to the wood. Local anaesthetic and a surgical procedure soon had them disconnected and sent on their way.

One case that stays with me involved a bank clerk whose job was to place cheques on a spike. While doing this she stabbed her hand and the spike went straight through. On her arrival we found the spike had entered the palm of her hand and protruded a couple of inches from the top while the wooden base held several cheques. X-ray showed no obvious bone damage and clinical examination suggested no major nerve or blood vessel damage. Accompanying the clerk was a bank official whose job was to retrieve the cheques as soon as the lady was freed. In the A&E theatre the doctor administered a local anaesthetic and then pulled the spike straight out. The wound was cleaned and dressed and antibiotics and tetanus injections were administered before discharge. I gave the spike (with all the cheques) to the official and he appeared more relieved at getting them back than enquiring how the clerk was.

* * *

Arena Essex raceway on the A1306 was primarily a speedway for stock car and dirt motorcycle races and so not surprisingly it provided us with an occasional customer or two. One day a stock-car driver came in unconscious after his car crashed through a barrier and turned over several times trapping him in his vehicle. On arrival, with his head bleeding, it was assumed his unconsciousness was due to a head injury. However later one of the St. John Ambulance crew commented on the way the incident had occurred. "That crash was really strange. The driver did not appear to even try to turn the car on the bend and he went straight through the crash barrier." Those details prompted the medical team to look further into what might be wrong. They discovered that the man must have had a bleed into his brain while driving and this caused him to black-out and crash. Treatment now focussed on the spontaneous bleed and the man was transferred to the neurosurgical unit at Oldchurch Hospital.

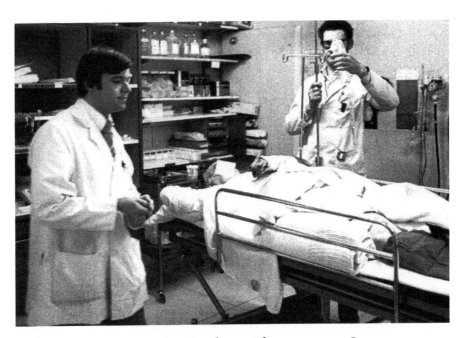

Treating a trauma patient in the accident room at Orsett

Another stock-car driver sustained horrendous ankle injuries but was very lucky as on that particular Sunday afternoon the A&E SHO on duty had orthopaedic experience. When the man arrived, we could see both his dislocated ankles were ripped open and the joints exposed. There was no blood supply to the feet. Immediately the doctor asked me to get a few instruments that would enable him to relocate the ankles into the sockets and hopefully restore the circulation. With me holding the right foot the doctor introduced the instruments into the open ankle joint and then, with a great deal of physical effort on his part, he relocated the ankle. The same procedure was applied to the left foot and with both feet and ankles now in the correct position, and with restored circulation, the orthopaedic team took the patient to the theatre.

The A13 was notorious for road traffic crashes and there was an accident black spot near the hospital - a bend known as 'Five Chimneys Corner'. The many incidents led to local people demanding double white lines or widening of the road. But drivers continued to overtake and head-on crashes were commonplace. Although it was compulsory to have front seat belts fitted to cars, the legislation to make wearing them compulsory did not come in until 1983. So during the 1970s and early 1980s severe facial injuries and chest injuries from head-on crashes were all too frequent. Many a nurse had to spend hours picking the glass fragments out of facial wounds.

My first encounter with a life-threatening chest injury was not from the A13 but a motorcyclist rounding the bend of a country lane and hitting a tree. When the 18-year-old arrived he was fully conscious and was able to tell us what had happened. He complained of localised chest pain on the right side and that area was bruised and very tender to any pressure. As he was breathless I administered oxygen and while the doctor was examining him, the patient suddenly grabbed at the oxygen mask and said: "I can't breathe." He then immediately suffered a respiratory and cardiac arrest. Resuscitation commenced with me providing chest compressions and another nurse ventilating using a bag and mask. The surgical registrar diagnosed a major chest injury (tension haemopneumothorax) and immediately inserted a chest drain. Blood poured from the drain faster than we could get the intravenous fluid into the man's vein. So much blood was pouring out that it just ran into a bucket and overflowed onto the floor. Within minutes resuscitation failed and the man was declared dead. Talking to the registrar afterwards, she said that the only way the man could have possibly survived was to have received a massive amount of intravenous blood and fluids combined with immediate chest surgery. In 1978 that was not feasible in our district general hospital and the whole concept of trauma care at that level was 15-20 years away.

* * *

During the late 1970s and the Winter of Discontent we experienced turbulent times with industrial action. On my birthday on 5th February 1979, dustmen who had already been working to rule came out on strike, and the next day ancillary staff at the hospital (members of the National Union of Public Employees) also started industrial action that was due to continue until mid-March. Ambulance staff also went on strike, and there were picket lines outside the entrances to the hospital. Although emergency cover was provided, by 16th February Orsett was only admitting emergency patients. Unlike the doctors' strike in 1975, this action did not close the hospital but it did cause chaos. Much of the cleaning and portering services were brought to a standstill and dirty linen and waste had to be removed from wards by nursing staff.

One of the more militant porters threatened to pull out all staff because I pushed a patient in a bed to X-ray. He told me I was breaking the strike by taking on portering duties. I replied that even when the porters were working normally nursing staff routinely pushed patients to X-ray and that I had no intention of stopping just to suit their strike. I heard no more from him.

Since returning to Orsett from Moorfields in 1975, I had reconnected with the RCN branch and had become the chair. I was able to help develop the local branch and ensure both professional and trade union matters were included in our regular business. Apart from the RCN, I had also continued my links with Grays Red Cross. I regularly went out to local fetes, carnivals, and craft shows and having been in the adult group since 16 I was now in a position to help teach. At weekends I invited the volunteers up to the department and with the co-operation of some staff, we would hold a mock incident, usually in a local car park or in the hospital grounds, then transport the 'injured' to the department. With the help of Rob Dodson (a Thurrock based ambulance man and friend) we put together a Red Cross Ambulance Training Programme, one of the first in Essex, and many of the volunteers undertook the course that was run over several weekends.

I knew most of the Essex ambulance staff and a few of us would meet up to play badminton and squash and one year entered the raft race at Southend-on-Sea. Fun was also important in the A&E department. We used to make up silly names on the A&E cards and many a nurse walked out to the waiting room to call for "Veronica Vomit" or some such, only to realise they'd been caught as no one got up from the chairs and the whole waiting room laughed. I was the victim of a prank when teddy bears were laid on trolleys and in the resuscitation room, making me think the department was very busy when in fact it was empty.

By July 1979 it was fifteen months since I had taken over the running of the department and I wanted the permanent staff to link more socially. Some of us already went out together for dinner and we were often at parties in the hospital. To get everyone together I started my BBQ's. Initially the events were small but they developed throughout the 1980s into major summer events with car treasure hunts during the afternoon and the BBQ in the evening.

Christmas celebrations for the staff were always difficult to organise as going out for dinner meant some staff inevitably missed out because they were on duty. So we came up with the idea of a Christmas party in the hospital for A&E staff, family and friends. I asked Miss O'Neill if we could use the outpatients waiting area in the late evening. With her agreement, our annual parties began. Several staff would contribute food and drink and because the area was so close to A&E, the staff on duty were able to take turns to join in.

The doctors' mess was a focal point for parties and by late evening/early hours of the next morning, the party spirit often got out of hand. One snowy winter's night we all decided to go outside and play snowballs. It was so cold that after a while someone had the brilliant idea of taking the snow inside so we could continue to play, but be in the warm. I can still see the snowman standing in the centre of the lounge and dozens of us having a snowball fight around him.

Christmas was also the opportunity for the hospital staff to hold a Christmas concert and we started rehearsals in October or November. The Christmas farce involved poems and songs depicting various members of staff; for example, an adaption of

'While Shepherds Watched Their Flocks By Night' began:

> While Charge Nurse Jones was sitting there in casualty one night, there came a call from Tilbury Docks, a ship had caught alight.
>
> "Fear not," said Ernst "for I am here and I will save them all. For my name is Pete and I've got big feet and a flashing light and all - Tra-la!"

And so it went on ……

* * *

Having appointed Mack and Diana as sisters with both having settled into their roles along with David and myself, I felt I had a strong senior team. By now I was happy with the way the department was progressing but felt there was so much more that could be achieved. Talking to one of the tutors from the school of nursing, she suggested I should look into applying for a travel scholarship and visiting A&E departments abroad.

Initially I dismissed the idea as I could not see myself being selected. But after some further thought, I decided to apply for a Florence Nightingale Travel Scholarship. To my astonishment I was invited to attend for interview so on 6th December 1979 I took the train to London and made my way to the Florence Nightingale Memorial Committee HQ at Grosvenor Crescent. I was so nervous I felt sick and at one point I considered walking back to the station and forgetting the whole thing. But I steeled myself to enter the building and soon found myself in front of three ladies asking probing questions. I had done my homework had contacted many of the departments and paramedic schools so that I could present an organised process. On leaving, I felt very positive but not convinced I would be successful.

On the 13th December, I received a letter from the committee informing me I had been awarded The Smith & Nephew Florence Nightingale Scholarship of £2,750. I could hardly believe it. And as if the award was not enough, Miss Trimble (DNO) was so pleased that a nurse from Orsett had won a national travel scholarship, she arranged for me to have the four months away as paid study leave.

My colleagues were so pleased and supportive and when I arrived in my office a few days later I found it festooned with cards, balloons and a large poster with a cartoon character (that was meant to be me) and the words 'Charge Nurse off to the USA'. Miss Trimble arranged for the Thurrock Gazette to interview me and take photographs so that everyone in the area would hear about my achievement. Now all I had to do was live up to the expectations.

In the early months of 1980 I made plans for the tour which would comprise three key areas:
1) In-hospital accident and emergency services.
2) The emergency nurse - extended training and records.
3) Pre-hospital care - the training and role of paramedics.

One of my main concerns was the travel logistics as I was visiting hospitals on both the east and west coasts of Canada and the USA. Mr Langley, manager of Harris Travel in Grays, took on the challenge with gusto. His professionalism was such that by the time I was ready to leave I even knew which daily bus I would catch in early September to travel from my hotel in Los Angeles to the paramedic school in Inglewood. He had also arranged travel across Canada by train.

Before I knew it July was approaching fast, though sometimes I wondered if the tour was ever going to happen. Letters to hospitals had gone astray, managers had changed and even when I was ready to leave the UK, a part of my tour in Pittsburgh was still to be confirmed.

12 HOW TRAUMA CARE SHOULD BE DONE

At 9.30pm a lady aged 26 was brought in to the emergency department of Mercy Hospital Pittsburgh with severe burns. She had been involved in a domestic argument and had been stabbed in her hip and both arms. She also had a laceration on her head. Petrol had been poured over her and she was set alight. On arrival she was responding to voice commands but she had third degree burns covering 80%-90% of her body. As I watched the trauma team in action I was impressed to see their speed and co-ordination as they attempted to save this lady's life.

She was intubated and ventilated. Numerous IV drips were set up, a catheter inserted into the bladder and a gastric tube into the stomach. Due to the depth and the way the burns encircled her body creating a tourniquet effect, escharotomies (large deep long cuts that slice through the burned skin) were performed to the chest, both legs, and both arms. This was something I had never seen done before and it was quite grotesque but essential if chest movement was to continue and limbs were not to be lost due to the increased pressure from the tissue swelling. Following a mass of tests and IV antibiotics, the patient was transferred to the burns unit.

The woman was just one of the many patients I encountered during my tour of emergency care in Canada and the USA. The four-month trip started on Sunday 6th July 1980. In Canada I visited three hospitals in Ontario, one in Vancouver and one on Vancouver Island. Even at this early stage I could see how advanced Canada was compared with our emergency care in the

UK. Assessment and triage of all patients on arrival by a registered nurse was commonplace, with initial treatment such as ice packs to muscle injuries and X-ray prior to seeing the doctor as the norm. Nursing documentation was produced for every patient and there was a trauma team system of patient care in every department, with trauma care co-ordinated across the Province.

McMasters Hospital emergency department in Hamilton, Ontario, was spacious and the waiting room had comfortable chairs, a colour television, piped music, daily newspapers and up-to-date magazines. Hamilton General, in the same Province, was old and cramped and had none of the luxuries seen in McMasters.

It was always my intention to see as much of Canada and the USA as possible so during one part of the trip I was able to visit Niagara Falls and take the train from Toronto to Vancouver. This journey took four days and three nights. My berth was private and although small in size, it contained a two-person couch, washbasin with drinking water and toilet. The double bed pulled down from the wall and almost completely filled the room. During the day, with the bed folded up, I was able to watch the countryside speed by as we travelled the width of Canada. At night, if I woke, I would look out of the window and see the change from well-lit streets to darkness across the plains.

Apart from routine emergency care, Vancouver General managed major mental health and drug problems. The department had psychiatric cells (that resembled prison cells) and, apart from a mattress on the floor, each cell was bare. Patients who were extremely agitated or aggressive would be sedated and strapped onto a trolley or placed in one of the cells. Violence was a problem mainly due to large numbers of patients being under the effects of alcohol or drugs. I saw this first hand when a young man arrived in a very agitated state. He was hallucinating and one of the staff told me he was 'a mushroom eater'. Magic mushrooms grew wild in the Province and so a high level of drug-related problems stemmed from the availability of these hallucinogenics.

Trauma care in British Columbia, like Ontario, was well co-ordinated. During the two weeks I was in Vancouver General, I saw a number of seriously injured people treated. The response to the arrival of one young man demonstrated the way trauma care was conducted.

Having received a call from the ambulance service following a road traffic accident the trauma room (theatre) was prepared and three trauma team nurses and the emergency department physician arrived. The patient was quickly assessed and trauma team doctors were called from other parts of the hospital. The man was unconscious and bleeding from both ears and mouth. Essential airway care and assisted breathing was quickly achieved. Intravenous fluids were started and X-rays ordered. Distension of the neck veins was observed, blood pressure was low and muffled heart sounds were heard.

It was suspected that the patient had blood around the heart and so drainage was undertaken (pericardiocentesis). Chest drains were inserted (due to a collapsed lung) as were oral gastric tubes and a urinary catheter. A blood transfusion commenced and the neurosurgeon ordered a CT scan and EEG which unfortunately showed no brain activity. On return from the scanner, it was decided to abandon further resuscitation measures. Although the outcome was unfortunate and not what was hoped for, I was very impressed with the way the whole team worked together and how both nurses and doctors had clear roles.

One of the main problems I observed in Vancouver was the amount of time patients spent in the department waiting for a hospital bed. Patients often waited several hours, and sometimes even days, before admission due to lack of beds. This was totally alien to me as at Orsett there was always a bed available and on the correct ward.

Shirley Stokes, the clinical instructor in Vancouver, not only provided me with a wealth of knowledge and documents, I also spent the weekend with her and her husband and recall sitting on their patio eating supper, drinking wine and watching the sun set over Vancouver Island and the Pacific Ocean.

The US part of the tour was far more dramatic and started in Seattle. Harbourview Medical centre had many challenges, again because of a large population with alcohol, drugs and psychiatric problems. It was the trauma centre for the Seattle and King County area. Like Canada, the department nursing supervisor had 24hr responsibility and managed all nursing staff. The unit was in an inner city location with high levels of social deprivation, and so a number of patients were arriving with complaints that were several weeks old. Many people presented with coughs, colds, flu and general ill health due to poor housing (or none) and poor nutrition. After triage, these patients were sent to a walk-in clinic rather than being seen in the emergency room.

There was an abundance of medical staff but due to the teaching aspect of the department, delays of one or two hours for non-life threatening conditions were the norm. Being the area psychiatric and alcohol misuse centre many of the patients had complex needs which meant the department was extremely busy.

Like Vancouver, as a result of the low bed capacity in the hospital, patients would wait hours for admission. Those with high blood alcohol levels were, by state law, referred to the detoxification centre (located in another unit in the county). Patients often waited 12 or more hours until sufficient numbers made transportation viable.

Due to the frequent violent episodes, security staff were permanently based in the department. After 8pm a security guard booked everyone in and out and policed the entrance to the department. This was my first encounter with such a large security presence which was certainly not a feature of the department at Orsett.

I learned very early on that Seattle had a well-organised response to cardiac arrest. I was told that as so many members of the public had basic resuscitation skills if someone collapsed in the street there would inevitably be someone ready to perform resuscitation. As many people told me, Seattle was the best place in the world to have a cardiac arrest, but the worst place to faint!

The paramedic programme combined with the fire service and ambulance staff resulted in a very efficient tiered response system. When a medical or trauma emergency was notified, fire trucks would be dispatched to the scene often arriving within five minutes. A paramedic ambulance would also be dispatched, usually arriving in seven or eight minutes.

Although much of the care was similar to Orsett, trauma care was far superior and the volume of trauma patients was unlike anything we had at Orsett. During one 11pm-7am shift I saw three patients with gunshot wounds, a road traffic victim, several patients suffering from a drug overdose, several assault victims and many patients suffering from psychiatric or alcohol-related illness. As well as all this, one man came in suffering a cardiac arrest and a helicopter brought in a lady with a severe head injury.

At one point during the night, all three patients with gunshot wounds were in the four-bedded trauma room at the same time. Although at Orsett we did get patients injured in fights at pubs or clubs, and we had the gunshot murder of Michael Toomey in 1976, I had never dealt with victims of violence on this scale.

The first man was a self-inflicted gunshot injury having accidentally shot himself in the leg. The second casualty was a young man who had been shot in the arm and chest during an argument. But it was the third person who was in the worst state.

He was a 16-year old who was found in bed with a married woman. The husband, having discovered the pair, laid the boy on the floor and shot him in the head. On arrival, the young man was unconscious. He had two intravenous infusions established at the scene by paramedics and his airway and breathing were by endotracheal tube and ventilation (also established by paramedics). As he arrived he had a cardiac arrest that responded to chest compressions and drugs. Urinary catheter and a gastric tube were inserted and all vital signs were recorded regularly and a blood transfusion commenced. An urgent CT scan was arranged and this showed several bullet fragments in his brain. The boy was taken to theatre. As often happens in emergency department work, I never did hear whether he made it.

Another night shift and the moon was full. Although I had never believed the full moon had a dramatic effect on some individuals, that night something definitely changed, and the number of patients with mental health issues increased substantially. I should have realised something was amiss the previous evening when I encountered some odd characters while returning from a harbourside restaurant. The steps to 1st Avenue were crowded with street dwellers acting very strangely indeed. It reminded me of the werewolf scene from Michael Jackson's Thriller video.

During my two weeks there, I was also fortunate to ride with the Medic One paramedic crew. Although it was a quiet day, we dealt with three victims from a hit and run incident on 1st Avenue. Fortunately, none of the three were severely injured. I also had the opportunity to visit the fire service dispatch centre. Compared with what we had in Essex this was state-of-the-art.

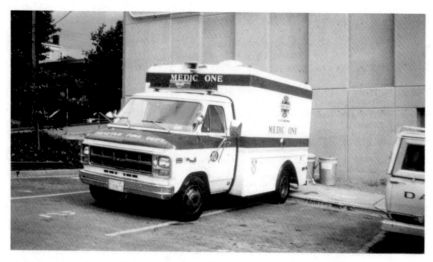

A paramedic vehicle in Seattle, one of many I rode in

The whole system was computerised so there was no turning little-coloured discs to show if an ambulance was in service here. All fire trucks and paramedic ambulances could be tracked by the computer and their exact location identified.

After a week of visiting the main tourist attractions of California, the Los Angeles part of my tour involved studying paramedic programmes and Winnie Hobbs, the programme director, ensured I saw all aspects of paramedic work and training. I was shown the communications centre located in the emergency department of the base hospital. This enabled paramedics to call in, telex ECGs to the department and ask a doctor for permission to carry out various procedures.

The first LA fire station I visited had one fire engine and one paramedic fire rescue truck. The latter was not designed to carry patients but conveyed paramedics and equipment to the scene.

For all calls, both vehicles were dispatched. During my day with the crew we had three calls and on the way back to the station we came across a driver with her car stuck on a railway crossing and a train arriving at any minute. By contacting the railway, the train was stopped and the vehicle pulled free. The following day it was busier with six calls though, apart from one patient, all the others were straightforward. What concerned me during one call was the distress of a mother who had no health insurance yet her child required emergency care. Before she would agree to the paramedics transferring her son to the hospital, they had to agree to take him to a unit that took welfare patients. This despite that hospital being further away from her home.

The second station I went to had a patient transport ambulance and the area it served was notorious for gang-related violence and drugs. On arrival at any call, especially to a house or flat, one paramedic would stand guard while the other treated the patient. I was told that on many occasions calls were a hoax to lure the crew into a house and then attack them and steal any drugs or other sellable items.

Our first call was to a known drug addict who was high on angel dust (PCP) and extremely agitated and violent. While one paramedic stood guard, I assisted the other with the patient. Our second call was classed as 'an incident' in a residential area. As we arrived, the paramedic spotted a man sitting on the front steps of the house with a rifle in his hands. I was told: "hit the deck" and as I lay on the floor of the ambulance, I could hear police sirens and helicopters above. Fortunately, the incident was rapidly dealt with and we returned to the station.

Leaving Los Angeles and heading for three weeks in Pittsburgh, I knew this part of my study tour was going to be very different. My placement was organised by Dr Ronald Stewart, the Director of the Centre for Emergency Medicine (CEM) and it involved time in the centre, paramedic units and observation in three emergency departments. The CEM had been set up in 1975 and was developing as a centre of excellence in the study and advancement of emergency care. As part of the University of Pittsburgh, the centre trained doctors in emergency medicine, organised and ran advanced courses for doctors and nurses in emergency care, carried out research and educated and clinically trained paramedics.

On the first afternoon I met with Ron's secretary who presented me with a vast array of reading material plus my itinerary. I participated in clinical lab work including intubation of airways on manikins and resuscitation. Then at 7pm I was treated to supper and arrived back at the residence at 1.30am.

Despite the late night, Ron expected me to be at Mercy Hospital on Saturday morning at 6am in the training suite where he was giving a talk to surgical teams on pre-hospital care. Following that, we returned to the centre ready for me to take part in the research he was conducting on Entonox, a gas mixture of 50% oxygen and 50% nitrous oxide. Although used routinely by ambulance crews and A&E departments in the UK, it was not routinely used in ambulances in Pittsburgh.

The research was designed to establish if paramedics would be exposed to Entonox while working in the ambulance. The study entailed Ron and I sitting inside an ambulance without ventilation all afternoon. As the ambulance drove around the city we both wore monitors to establish any exposure to Entonox when using it in a closed space. It was extremely hot and at one point the research was temporarily halted so we could have an ice cream. Arriving back at the residence at 6pm I had a quick shower and change before we went out to a Japanese restaurant. Returning to my room at 12.15am I recorded in my diary: "This place is unbelievable, such friendliness and everyone so welcoming. I feel very much a part of it. Ron Stewart lives for the centre and his work".

Although my programme included visits to three departments and specific clinical training in intubation, defibrillation, and intravenous cannulation, I was also booked to attend a range of lectures. On Monday morning I was up at 7am and went across to the emergency department for a lecture with medical and nursing staff on rashes. From there I travelled to Mercy Hospital in downtown Pittsburgh. The city did not have a designated trauma centre so all three main hospitals took trauma victims. Mercy Hospital was a large unit in a very violent area so security was not only provided by security staff but they had their own hospital police with a small police station on site (part of the main city police service). Security and police personnel continuously monitored patients in the emergency room waiting area.

Elsewhere on the tour I had the weekends free, but this was not the case in Pittsburgh. Ron had organised my first visit to the Presbyterian University Hospital's emergency department for

Saturday afternoon/evening. I arrived and met with three of the nurses who discussed nursing care and I spent time observing their work. Ensuring I was kept busy, after leaving the department at 10pm I met with Ron at the centre. I helped him prepare for the Great Race that was being held in Pittsburgh the following day. As I left at 11.30pm, Ron was still working away.

I was up at 6am on Sunday, ready to arrive at Medic Command and leave for Point State Park by 7.45am to join the medical and paramedic cover for the race. I was located in the medic post at the finish line. About 12,000 runners were expected and as some had suffered cardiac arrests in the previous year nothing was being left to chance. Fortunately, no serious incidents occurred and we were finished by midday.

On Monday at 8am I began a full day learning how to intubate. Ron lectured in the morning and in the afternoon we practised on manikins and anaesthetised pigs. As the practical session progressed, the position of the manikin became harder. When we were taken to a laboratory where the pigs were lying on trolleys I was astounded by the sight and could not believe it was acceptable. In groups, we were allocated a pig. As this animal's upper airway was considered the closest to the human, we now had to demonstrate intubation of the pig. The day finished in the late afternoon and plans were made for me to take an exam the following Friday. If I were successful, I would link up with an anaesthetist and spend some time during the final week in theatres under supervised practice. In addition to the intubation course, I also had classroom training in intravenous cannulation with skill development planned for the final week.

During the next week, I visited the children's emergency department, attended numerous lectures and rode with paramedics. Any free time I had was spent as a tourist in the city. On Friday I attended a CPR session and then sat the written and practical exam for intubation and CPR. To my delight I passed both. Despite a busy day by 4pm I left for another shift at Mercy ER finishing at 11.30pm.

As my final week approached, I had been so busy and learned so much that my head was spinning. The following two days were going to be spent in the operating theatre where I could now intubate patients under the supervision of the nurse anaesthetist (not a position known in the UK). I also joined the IV team touring Presbyterian Hospital changing or inserting new IV cannulas. The period on the oncology unit really tested my ability to identify veins suitable for cannulation. These patients had had numerous cannulas and IV drugs, so finding a suitable vein was a challenge, but one that I relished, as I knew it would help on my return to Orsett.

Ron Stewart was an inspiration to me and even on my last day he had me interpreting ECG rhythms and studying for competency in manual defibrillation. My final achievement was a pass in that workshop. Passing all three skills (intubation, cannulation, and defibrillation) was going to enable me, on return home, to qualify as a Registered Emergency Medical Technician (REMT). This was a major step forward for my plans to help develop extended nursing skills in A&E at Orsett and the paramedic role with Essex Ambulance Service.

Unlike anywhere else on my visit, the Maryland Institute for Emergency Medical Services Systems (MIEMSS) was a complete statewide emergency service which included pre-hospital as well as hospital services. The shock-trauma hospital was at the centre of it all and that was where I would be spending most of my time. I was able to attend a two-day trauma course, a two-day cardiac care course and I also rode out in one of the paramedic vehicles.

The shock-trauma centre was opened in 1961 and grew from a two-bedded area into a 56-bedded centre. It only received patients with multi-system life-threatening injuries. The centre included an admitting area, plus critical care, intensive care and intermediate care areas. In addition, a neurological unit had just opened. At the entrance was a large framed picture of Albert

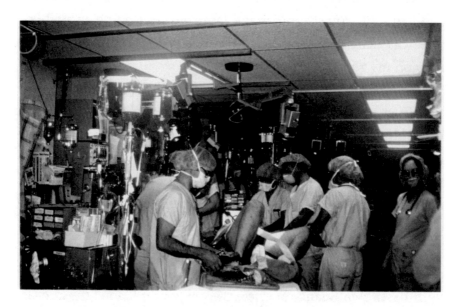

The MIEMSS team in action in 1980

Einstein with one of the brilliant physicist's quotations that really summed up this extraordinary unit's ethos:

'Great spirits have always encountered violent opposition from mediocre minds'

Most of my time was spent in the first floor admitting area, where there were six trolley bays. Each bay looked like something from Star Trek's USS Enterprise. I had never seen so much equipment around one trolley. There were ventilators, ceiling mounted IV poles, monitoring equipment, trays for all manner of emergency procedures and a fridge containing 0-negative blood. The operating theatres were adjacent to the admitting area and X-rays were performed from machines fixed on ceiling gantries. The centre dealt with approximately 1500 patients per year, 60% arriving by helicopter. The centre had an 80% survival rate.

When a patient was en route to the centre the main control would broadcast a loud PA message announcing the imminent arrival. The helipad was on the roof of the multi-storey car park directly opposite the centre. When a helicopter was due to arrive, an ambulance would drive up to the roof of the car park and a doctor and nurse would also attend.

In the admitting area, the team would start to prepare the bay. IV lines would be run through with plasma (that was the main IV fluid used in this facility), packs would be opened and the progress of the arrival was broadcast from the PA system: "Arrival in five minutes." Once the helicopter landed the doctor and nurse would assess the patient, stabilise them if needed then transfer them to the ambulance as rapidly as possible. With bells ringing throughout the car park warning drivers to keep clear, the ambulance would drive to the centre entrance. During the short journey, the doctor would be attending to the patient's airway while the nurse cut all clothing away and performed a ninety-second full body assessment. From the entrance, the patient was wheeled along the corridor, up in the lift to the admitting area.

Once the patient (now naked and covered with a blanket) was on the trolley they disappeared under a sea of medical and nursing staff, all working in a coordinated way. Spinal immobilisation, established in the helicopter, would be reviewed and maintained until spinal X-rays were taken. Doctors established various IV lines and tubes would be inserted into bladder and nose. Depending on the airway and breathing, intubation and ventilation would be carried out. If necessary, a mini-laparotomy (small incision into the abdomen) would be performed to enable a peritoneal lavage (fluid infused in and suctioned out of the abdomen) to see if any blood was present. The radiographer automatically X-rayed neck, spine, pelvis and any injured limbs. Chest X-rays were normally taken with the individual rapidly lifted into a sitting position (X-ray checking for any fluid in the chest or around the heart) then the patient was rapidly laid back flat (I had not seen this method of chest X-ray performed anywhere else). If required, blood would be administered in individual components rather than whole units. Arterial lines allowed measurement of arterial pressure and facilitated blood specimens for blood gas analysis. CT scan was available and the patient was then rapidly transferred to the operating theatre.

To take advantage of this extraordinary facility during my three weeks I worked both day and night shifts. I also spent a day in the large critical care unit where I met patients who had suffered appalling injuries yet survived. One patient who I accompanied to the nuclear medicine department was having a test to determine the integrity of the heart's ventricular wall and septum. She had suffered a gunshot injury and the bullet had injured the liver, hit bone and ricocheted into the heart piercing the septum.

During my period of observation in the admitting area, I saw 10 patients with multi-system trauma. I cannot describe the adrenaline rush as I stood on the rooftop heliport at three in the morning. Looking out over the lights of Baltimore I would scan the night sky and spot the lights of the helicopter, and then hear the sound of the propeller. Even though the shock-trauma nurse and doctor were there, my heart rate would increase in anticipation. How injured would the patient be? Could life be saved? On one night alone we received three major trauma victims, and they were no sooner admitted when three more arrived. One man had been shot twice, causing severe injuries to his neck, eye, and face.

Despite several visits to the institute both day and night, I was always overwhelmed by the way so many patients benefited from one of the world's most advanced trauma centres. And not just the patients. Immediately relatives arrived in the centre a social worker would be linked with the family. Very often there was disbelief, denial, and anger. For most families there were weeks or even months not knowing if their loved ones would survive. And even if they did, the whole family needed constant support during the rehabilitation stage, and always hanging over them was the fear that the health insurance may run out or did not cover certain aspects of the care.

Rehabilitation of severely injured people was an important part of the centre's work. As patients progressed from critical to intensive care, and then to intermediate care, so the rehabilitation program developed. Once discharged there was also an outpatient service, though for many because they lived in other parts of the state, this care would be provided locally.

Baltimore was not far from Washington DC and New York so during my time off I visited both. As my study tour drew to an end it was time to reflect on some of the positive and negatives I had observed. Violence in some of the cities continuously spilled over into the emergency departments creating the need for security staff and even hospital police. Also, the level of violence with guns and knives was horrific.

Beds were in short supply in many hospitals and this led to long waiting times for many patients requiring admission. It was common to see many patients nursed overnight in the emergency department. Seeing nurses providing bed baths and ordering breakfast, lunch and dinner for patients in emergency was totally alien to me. This congestion caused knock-on problems for new patients arriving, temporary holding areas had to be created in corridors and overall waiting times for all patients increased.

But the way trauma care was organised and the trauma team

system worked was impressive. Seeing a team of doctors and nurses working in a systematic way certainly improved the outcome. The concept of identified trauma centres with all specialities on one site was something I had always hoped for in the UK. Major incidents were well co-ordinated with one hospital being the designated lead and linking others through radio contact.

The majority of nurses working in emergency departments had previously worked in critical care areas and many had advanced life support and trauma training. All had one or two years post-registration experience. Detailed six to nine week induction and on-going training programmes were in place. What we in the UK called extended skills were normal activities for the emergency nurses. These included siting IV lines, manual defibrillation, intubation and many other clinical procedures that enabled the nursing and medical staff to work as a team.

Triage was also very advanced. The sorting and prioritising of patients improved care for the most seriously ill or injured patient. A nurse saw every patient in the waiting room and immediate intervention such as ice packs to injured limbs could be initiated. The approach to all nursing care was a structured assessment, including the nurse, if necessary, sending the patient to X-ray rather than waiting for the doctor. This was definitely something I wanted to introduce at Orsett.

Nursing documentation was a very positive aspect of the emergency nursing care. The length and complexity of the nursing records varied considerably and although sometimes rather long, the idea of nurses recording their assessment and intervention was also something I was determined to bring back to Orsett.

The paramedic service, compared to the UK ambulance service in 1980, was far superior. The systems were very different in each area I had visited, with the length and complexity of the training varying considerably. The assessment and interventions by paramedics meant patients were more stable, and treatment had commenced before arriving at the hospital. Although most systems required the paramedic to call the emergency department and obtain medical direction, the reality was the paramedic was often far more aware of what was required and had often intervened before any direction from the doctor. My only concern was the length of time some patients were kept at the scene before being transported, what was often referred to by the emergency department staff as 'stay and play'.

I finished my study tour with a two week holiday in Miami and then, once home, having produced a report for the Florence Nightingale Committee, I later had two articles published in *Nursing Mirror*, one entitled 'A&E in USA-OK?' and the other called 'Music While You Wait'. In those two articles, I reflected on my visits and highlighted some of the changes my study tour led to at Orsett, as well as other changes I had proposed for the Essex ambulance service and emergency nursing in the UK.

13 THE RISE OF PARAMEDICS IN THE UK

The development of the Association of Emergency Medical Technicians (AEMT) in 1978 triggered the move to paramedic training in the UK. In Thurrock some of the ambulance staff, led by Rob Dodson, were keen to expand their knowledge and skills and formed a local AEMT branch. Invited to join and help develop the ambulance staff we would meet at Rob's home and that started what was to be a very long journey to improve patient care.

Initially, I taught the ambulance staff a whole range of skills and supported these with appropriate knowledge. As AEMT became more established throughout Essex, consultants Peter Ernst from Orsett, and Janet Porter from Southend, gave up their time to teach. By 1981 discussions were being held with the Essex Ambulance Service on the possibility of some staff starting intravenous lines and intubating the patient's airway (I&I). Due to my AEMT links and my studies of the paramedic programmes in Canada and the US, I was invited to become a member of the emerging Essex Ambulance Extended Training Advisory Group (the word paramedic was not in use at that time as the extended skills would be limited). The group became fully established in 1982 and I remained a member of this committee until 1998.

As the group expanded and included a consultant anaesthetist from Chelmsford, I was heavily involved in developing the training programs as well as training the ambulance staff. These programmes were linked into the National Paramedic programme so it is fair to say that work from Essex had a direct link to the development of paramedic training in the UK.

The first group of ambulance personnel undertook their I&I training at Orsett, Southend and Chelmsford hospitals and study sessions moved from Rob's house into the ambulance training school in Chelmsford. We used to drive there from Thurrock and then after training (normally around 10pm) we would stop off at one of the local pubs for something to eat and drink. The group became a very social gathering as well developing the first Registered Emergency Medical Technicians (REMT) in Essex.

At the same time as we were building up the local training in Essex, in 1981 I was contacted by the national AEMT and to my astonishment was invited to join the national committee. I felt honoured and surprised as I had never dreamt that others would have heard about my study tour. From 1982, this AEMT group became the National Paramedic Development Group and in 1989 the Joint Royal Colleges Advisory Group. It took forward the National Training Programme (much of which originated from the early Essex extended skills training) enabling individuals to become paramedics.

In 1987, the first journal for emergency medical technicians was published, Emergency Care, and the editor was Yvonne McEwen, the nurse who inspired me in 1984 to run for office in the RCN A&E forum.

At the national level, I was now meeting the key players from a number of other ambulance services and doctors who were members of the national committee of BASICS. One of the early requests I had was to help establish a link between AEMT and the RCN A&E committee. Although I had become a local A&E member of the South East Thames Accident Group, in 1982 I had never met any members of the national committee. A meeting was arranged at RCN headquarters in London and two AEMT committee members and I met with the A&E committee. It was a disastrous meeting. None of the A&E committee showed any interest in paramedic training; in fact, some were hostile to the idea of paramedics, full stop. The view was that the ambulance service conveys and the doctors and nurses treat. Fortunately, it was not long before views started to change and emergency nurses and ambulance staff began working together.

Being asked to present some lessons from my Canadian/USA tour to the AEMT national conference in Burton-on-Trent in December 1981, I was aware I had never spoken at any conference before, let alone a national conference. When the day came the country was covered in snow. Despite this we drove up to the venue and I remember changing into my suit from the jeans and jumper I had worn in case we needed to dig the car out of a snowdrift. The conference was in the postgraduate centre. The heating had failed and as the day progressed it was getting colder by the minute. By the time I was due to go on the audience was cold and restless. My legs would not stop shaking and I am not sure how much was fear and how much was the cold. I had a number of slides to show and I did my best to make the talk interesting. My own rating was 'could have done better' and I was not sure if I ever wanted to go through that experience again.

National AEMT meetings were held in Peterborough Hospital under the chairmanship of Dr Robin Glover, A&E consultant. They were always fascinating and as a body, we were moving the whole process of paramedic development forward. One meeting in April 1982 took on an additional significance as one of our committee members who represented the Navy, told us he was waiting for an important telephone call and may have to leave. He could not say why. As the meeting progressed the naval officer's pager went off. He disappeared and soon returned with a concerned face as he told us he had to leave immediately. We all wondered if it related to the ongoing troubles in the Falkland Islands. What we did not know was that on the previous evening the prime minister, Margaret Thatcher, had given the go-ahead for a taskforce to be assembled. The day after our meeting Argentinian forces invaded the Falklands and the taskforce set sail on Monday 5th April 1982.

Having had the opportunity to link with so many national leaders in the world of emergency medicine, I was privileged to be invited in 1985 to play a part in the fourth World Congress on Emergency and Disaster Medicine held in Brighton (the first time the Congress had taken place in the UK). The guest of honour, HRH Princess Anne, conducted the opening ceremony and then we all stood on the seafront as the Red Arrows performed an impressive air display. During the four-day event we heard from some 200 contributors from 28 countries on all aspects of emergency and disaster care including prevention, planning, and intervention.

* * *

As the years progressed, in Essex as well as nationally, advanced ambulance training became well established and many of the early advanced ambulance practitioners were involved in training new recruits. I continued my role on both the local and national committee as well as my teaching and examining work. The advisory committees continued to grow with many more medical staff from backgrounds other than A&E. Monitoring equipment in the ambulances was increasingly used and the advanced roles continued to develop. In September 2010, while visiting the ambulance station and training department at Basildon, I took the opportunity to look inside one of the latest vehicles and it reminded me of the paramedic ambulances I had ridden in during my travel scholarship in 1980. It was a delight to see how the ambulance service had developed and was especially rewarding for me to know I had played a part in it.

14 TURBULENT TIMES

The 1980s were a period of change for me professionally and personally. I bought a timeshare villa in Malta, I found new interests like attending motorbike and rock music events. I took up judo, skiing and holidaying on narrow boats. As a family, we suffered the sadness of watching my Nan, a strong loving lady, succumb to senile dementia. She died in 1987.

I fell in love with Linda, we became engaged and even booked the church and reception for our wedding. Although a strong relationship developed there were also disagreements, and despite our best attempts we realised it was not going to work. I accept much of the blame because I was possibly too obsessed with my work so, despite our love for each other, we sadly decided to part.

I continued to be very active in the Grays Red Cross Centre, enjoying all aspects of the voluntary work. Much to my surprise in December 1982, I was awarded the Voluntary Medical Service Medal for long and efficient service to the British Red Cross Society. Then in April 1983 I was awarded the Badge of Honour and Life Membership of the Red Cross.

Professionally I was active in the local RCN branch and in 1982 joined the RCN South East Thames Accident Group. In May 1983 I attended my first national A&E conference. This changed my professional life significantly as I was asked to join the planning committee for the first International A&E conference, to be held in 1985. I was also invited to become a member of the

Receiving the Red Cross Voluntary Medical Services Medal from Norman Shearman, director of Thurrock Red Cross

Photo: Thurrock Gazette

editorial board of the forum's newsletter Emergency Nurse.

At the 1984 A&E conference, a keynote speaker, Yvonne McEwen (a nurse disaster specialist from Scotland) gave a challenging speech and rallied all delegates to fight for A&E nursing. She called on nurses to press for more autonomy, to stop being the handmaidens of doctors and to prove the nurse can provide excellent care to the patient. I took up the challenge and in 1985, I was elected the RCN A&E forum's public relations officer.

Having returned to Orsett towards the end of November 1980 I decided to reflect on my tour over the next month. I was focussed on what I had gained from the experience and how it could improve the care we provided at Orsett. Also, I reflected on how what I had learned about paramedic programmes could feed into AEMT and the Essex Ambulance Service.

I set about making the simple changes first and then began working towards the more challenging improvements over the next year or two. On the minor injuries side, I introduced the ice machine and we ensured that every patient who had a strain or sprain would have ice packs applied while waiting to see the doctor. Although the ice machine produced sufficient ice for the minor injuries we still had to rely on the local pub in the village to provide ice for when we needed to pack an amputated limb for transfer to the plastic surgeons. One young lad of 14 years amputated his hand while in a metal work class at school. Fortunately it was a clean amputation and the plastic surgeons successfully reattached his hand with excellent results.

In the waiting room, I persuaded a local charity (Hospital Friends) to purchase a tape player and speakers so we could have music. Meanwhile on the major side of the department, I wanted to improve trauma care. Peter Ernst was supportive but on-call surgical/orthopaedic teams had just one registrar and two housemen (junior doctors), so the idea of a trauma team as I had seen in the US and Canada was many years away. What I could change were the facilities and nursing input. I discussed with the staff the idea of using the theatre as the main trauma/ resuscitation room and with some new equipment this would improve the service. Change did not come easily to everyone. Miss O'Neill, on the request of the night nursing officer, wanted the change to the theatre and accident room reversed. After a heated discussion, I won the argument and retained the changes.

In the 1970s and early 1980s it was common practice in most A&E departments for walk-in patients, with what appeared to be a minor injury, to book in at reception and (as long as they were not bleeding all over the floor) they were sent to the waiting room. No clinical staff saw the patient until they were called in to see the doctor.

One winter's day many people were slipping on ice and snow so the department was very busy with people suffering from limb injuries. The waiting room was full and waiting times to see the doctor were long. I called a lady through and she told me she had fallen and injured her wrist. She had a thick winter jacket on with sleeves that had elasticated wrists. As I gently helped her remove the jacket I saw she had an open fracture and the bone was protruding through the skin. I was appalled that this lady had waited so long with such a major injury. The risk to her hand and overall health was high. I decided there and then that the initial assessment system I had observed during my tour had to be introduced.

Over the next couple of weeks, I discussed my ideas for immediate assessment with the staff. I asked the nurses to provide a quick assessment of the injury and then put the card in the cue. As the majority of nurses in that area were students, I was happy for them to assess the patient, as this was better than the current system.

The majority of the staff complied and only one senior colleague continued to use the old system. I decided to return to the department after going off duty and call in on my days off to catch him out. It did not take many such visits before the staff member complied. Over the next couple of years, the system was refined including the development of a number of ink stamps with printed key assessment criteria to stamp on patients' cards.

During 1983/84 we introduced a formal triage system. With the support of Peter Ernst, I introduced four priority categories and linked maximum waiting times to see the doctor to each one. Priority one was immediate, priority two within 30 minutes, priority three within 1 hour, and priority four any time afterwards. Peter and I developed a guide to help staff determine which patients went into each category. Training of staff was organised and the system started. Although not the first department to introduce this system, we were one of few departments at that time with such an organised approach.

Although I had introduced the ink stamps to the minor injuries area, I had not moved to introducing nursing documentation for the majors' side. This was something for the future; however, events meant it happened earlier than I had anticipated. One of the senior lecturers from the school of nursing came to see me about the nursing methodology that was being used in the school. He insisted that if students were to continue to come to A&E we had to be using the nursing process and the paperwork that went with it.

When I was shown the proposed paperwork, it was clearly

unsuitable for the department. I challenged the senior tutor to spend a shift in the department and to use the nursing process and the paperwork in the way he had suggested. He agreed and came to work in the department and after some time we reviewed progress. I pointed out that while he had completed his assessment of one patient I had assessed three, and the doctor had already seen two of those.

There needed to be a compromise and that is when my second simple A4 sheet was introduced (the first being the care plan on ward 3). This sheet enabled the nurses to record their assessment of the patient, maintain a record of the nursing interventions and record an evaluation. I deliberately kept it to one side of A4 so it was simple to use and not time-consuming. The last thing I wanted was nurses spending more time on documentation and less time with the patient. For now, everyone was happy, but things would change again after 1986.

Year on year accident and emergency departments were getting busier and Orsett was no exception. Clinically I was still a part of the nursing rota and one morning I drove into the recreation ground car park as usual. As I got out of the car, I saw a man slumped in the bushes. He was conscious but confused and had a bandage on his leg. I discovered he had been there most of the night. I told him to stay where he was and went to the department for a wheelchair. I pushed him into the A&E and the night staff informed me he had walked out before his treatment was completed and they had no idea he had simply bedded down in the car park.

One of our regulars was George, a chap in his 70s who came in one day with a very infected wound to his thumb. He was a loud but friendly man and slightly eccentric. During his numerous follow-up visits, the wound became worse rather than better. Necrotising fasciitis, commonly known as 'flesh-eating disease' was considered but tests showed no specific cause. It reached a point where the whole thumb was full of rotting flesh and pus. The wound dressing was getting larger on each visit. At one stage, amputation was considered but eventually, the thumb did heal, albeit as an abnormal non-functional thumb. Lacking in some social graces, George would see me in Grays High Street and shout down the road "Hello nurse. My thumb's still hanging on." It reached the stage that when I saw him coming I would duck into any shop and hide behind a shelving unit until he had passed.

John had been coming into the department with his asthma for many months. He became well-known to all the staff and despite getting the correct treatment, he would often have a respiratory arrest, be ventilated, go to the intensive care unit and the next morning have his breakfast and go home.

One evening John arrived in the life-threatening stage of an asthmatic attack. As we started his ventilation, he suddenly went into cardiac arrest. I began chest compressions and noticed after a few compressions the pressure in his chest was increasing. He had a tension pneumothorax so I informed the locum medical registrar who was in charge of the resuscitation. But he continued to focus on the arrest from a medical viewpoint rather than treating the air building up in John's chest. Fortunately,

Peter Ernst was in the department so I asked one of the staff to get him to come immediately. Once Peter arrived, he inserted a cannula into John's chest then a chest drain.

Unfortunately, despite our efforts, John died. As we had got to know him and his wife over many years, the staff were devastated - it was like losing a friend. I had nurses in tears and despite my own feelings, I was desperately trying to stay in control. Telling John's wife was very difficult and once she had left, I told the staff I needed to go over to the sterile supply department to replace some of the equipment. When I got in there I felt very emotional and, now alone, I burst into tears. Several weeks after John's death a hospital colleague told me that his wife was overwhelmed by the reaction of the staff. She had not realised how much John meant to them until she saw them crying and that had helped her during the early weeks after his death.

Another of our 'customers' was Ben. It would have been better for Ben not to keep extremely poisonous fish as he had been stung by them on more than one occasion. One day he arrived in the department almost at death's door. The antidote was only available in one of the London hospitals, so when he came in we stabilised him while a police car was despatched to deliver the antidote. It was like a scene from an action movie, with a staff member standing at the entrance as a police car with sirens wailing and blue lights flashing arrived and the antidote to save Ben's life was handed over. The nurse rushed into the resus room, vial in hand and the doctor administered the drug. Now, would it work? It always had done and it did on this occasion.

Despite warnings of the risk to his life, Ben insisted on keeping the fish and we would see him again and again. Until one year he did not get to us on time.

Glen had sustained a serious head injury and his condition was deteriorating. Results from X-rays and a detailed clinical examination led to diagnosis of an extradural haematoma (a blood clot just below the skull that was pressing on the brain). Although the surgical registrar had spoken with the neurological team at Oldchurch Hospital, and transfer had been agreed, it was clear he was not going to survive the journey. As the decline was so rapid, the surgical registrar decided to operate in our resuscitation room and release the clot. Once the man was anaesthetised the registrar incised the scalp to create a skin flap. With a drill and bit that resembled the one my dad used to drill wood, he started to turn the drill and the bit cut into the skull. Through the borehole, blood started oozing out and with gentle suction the clot was removed. Glen was then admitted to intensive care and following a long recovery was discharged home.

Although many outcomes in our resuscitation room were successful sadly others were not. One lady, who came in with cancer of the neck and throat, with a tumour eating into one of the major blood vessels in her neck, had a very poor prognosis. The lady was fully conscious and knew the likely outcome. Her husband was with her and I stood back as they held each other's hands. All the ENT doctor and I could do was wait. I kept replacing the blood-soaked dressing on her neck until it was clear that at any minute the carotid artery would burst. I persuaded the husband to step outside while the lady, still fully conscious, was given morphine as the carotid artery gave way. She drifted into a peaceful sleep and then stopped breathing. That was undoubtedly one of the most traumatic experiences of my career and one I hoped never to repeat.

* * *

Steve's wife was dysfunctional and, like him, relied heavily on drugs and alcohol. I had known Steve since my time on nights in 1975. Social services had tried to help the couple keep their small child but the evening they were 'stoned' and set fire to the flat was when it was decided to take the child into care.

The three of them were brought in but fortunately none had suffered burns or smoke inhalation. Knowing how Steve would react to his child being removed, I quickly sent a staff nurse with the child down to X-ray and asked for them to be locked in a room. When told by the social services that the child was being taken into care, Steve went wild and chased around the department searching for the youngster. Crashing around and throwing open doors, he wreaked havoc. Police were called and a very traumatic event was played out as Steve fought with the police, while the wife screamed abuse at all of us, and the staff nurse was locked in the room with the child. Once the police had removed Steve and his wife, I unlocked the room, social services took the child into care, and the staff nurse had a well-earned cup of tea.

* * *

On one occasion as I was returning from a split shift, there was a young lad in the accident room with superficial scalds to his body. As I walked in I was met with what could only be described as a steam room. Saline was pouring like a waterfall from the patient trolley, the room was flooded and there was the staff nurse pouring more litres of saline over the young man.

I was furious and immediately told her to stop. I went to fetch a dry trolley and asked the man to move over onto it. He was shouting: "Keep pouring." I said no and moved him to another room. Having covered his scalds with green surgical towels and making sure he had pain relief, I returned to the staff nurse in the accident room. "He kept screaming he wanted the saline over his scalds so I just kept pouring, and the doctor said to carry on." I looked at the dozens of empty litre saline bottles. The pharmacy must have been almost emptied and most of it was now all over the floor. So much so I had to get the cleaners to use suction powered machines to remove it.

"Did common sense not tell you this was a ridiculous situation?" I asked her. "Did you not realise with the central heating and all that fluid you were just making things worse?" I told her to go off duty and as she trudged up the corridor in her soaking uniform with her cap collapsed on her head, angry as I was, I couldn't help thinking she looked a very comical figure.

15 PLANNING FOR WHEN DISASTER STRIKES

In 1983, Mr Gonzalez (the district nursing officer) offered me the role of nursing officer for A&E with 24-hour accountability and management of the nursing staff. The day and night nursing officers would relinquish their management of A&E. I immediately accepted.

As I was a clinically based nursing officer it gave me the opportunity to take on the increased responsibilities of managing the nursing staff and the department, and also remain on the duty rota and continue to nurse patients on a regular basis.

My first battle was to stop the ongoing practice of moving one of the two night nurses away from A&E when wards were busy. This had annoyed me ever since I had been on nights as a staff nurse in 1975/6 and although I won the battle, this did not go down well with the night nursing officer.

While I was working in my office on a Saturday afternoon, I saw a lady run across from the main hospital doors towards the department. Seeing her distress, I left the office and met her at the ambulance entrance. "Come quickly," she said, "my mum is dying. The nurse needs help." As I arrived I could see an elderly lady in the passenger seat of a car. She'd had a cardiac arrest as she was being discharged from hospital. With help from the nurse who had brought the lady down from the ward we got her out onto the pavement and I started resuscitation. Sending the nurse across to A&E, I told her to summon the doctor and other staff to the incident. The doctor and the other nurses and I between us carried out full resuscitation on the pavement. While getting the lady onto a stretcher trolley and back to the department, I was able to talk to the nurse from the ward. The lady was being discharged but was known to have terminal cancer. Once we had established this from the patient's notes, we abandoned any further resuscitation attempts.

* * *

Although mishaps with stretcher trolleys were commonplace in comedy sketches, the day a patient rolled off the ambulance stretcher trolley was anything but a funny episode. We had received a call to expect a patient in cardiac arrest. As was the norm, I called the arrest team and went to the entrance doors to receive the patient. The ambulance arrived and during the unloading, one of the crew must have lifted slightly higher on one side of the stretcher than the other. The next thing was the patient rolled from the stretcher onto the road. I immediately continued resuscitation while the ambulance crew repositioned the trolley and then all three of us lifted the man back on the stretcher. Now well positioned he was wheeled to the resuscitation room.

Once the arrest was dealt with and all was well with the patient, one of the doctors asked why it had taken so long from the ambulance arrival to getting the man in the resuscitation room. As I told the story, I could see smiles beginning and then everyone burst into laughter. That may sound uncaring but, in reality, humour is how many nurses and doctors cope, hence the popularity of such films as Carry on Nurse or Carry on Doctor.

A further mishap with a trolley occurred when I was preparing a patient for a general anaesthetic. The lady had a dislocated shoulder and we had tried all the regular practices including hanging her arm over the edge of the trolley, some mild sedation to get muscle relaxation but nothing had worked. It was decided to relocate the shoulder under general anaesthetic and as I went to lay the lady flat I lost control of the top end of the trolley and she shot into a flat position. With the force from the action, her shoulder relocated. Although not an acceptable way to relocate a shoulder she was very pleased that no anaesthetic was required.

* * *

Dave worked at Coryton oil refinery in a plant using hydrofluoric acid which is extremely dangerous. A burn can cause death as it extracts calcium from the body. He sustained a significant burn (slightly larger than his palm) and the refinery medical staff had started treatment by irrigating the area and then using calcium gel. In the A&E department, we had a special cupboard with all the antidote gel, tablets, and injections. All the staff were aware of the need to intervene quickly. On arrival, the area of injury was assessed and the gel treatment continued. Due to the size of the burn, calcium tablets were given and calcium was injected under the burn. Blood calcium levels were checked, intravenous fluids started and cardiac monitoring initiated. Regular blood calcium was monitored and calcium injections were given intravenously to maintain normal body levels. Once stable Dave was admitted to the intensive care unit and on-going monitoring continued until his calcium levels were normal.

On another evening I was working on majors when an inexperienced ambulance attendant came in and reported they had a lady with a small wound on her abdomen. The ambulance attendant assured me the lady was reasonably OK. I asked them to take her over to minors but when the crew wheeled her in, I took one look at her and immediately diverted them to majors. She was pale, cold and clammy - typical signs of shock. The so-called small wound was, in fact, a stab wound penetrating into the lady's abdomen above her liver. Potentially she could have had a life-threatening internal bleed, yet externally she did just have, as I was told, a small wound on her abdomen.

* * *

The morning I arrived on duty to be told a tugboat had been rammed by a larger ship and sunk in the Thames was the beginning of a very busy shift. The night staff were attempting to resuscitate one of the crew and three others were suffering from hypothermia. Having relieved the night staff we continued to attempt resuscitation on the man and care for the others with blankets and warm drinks. Knowing there were still other men trapped in the tug, the ambulance service requested the mobile team to be available on the quayside of Tilbury landing stage.

Although we always responded to such requests, I only had two other registered nurses with me, one of whom was only starting work in the department that morning. I also had the follow-up clinic to organise and we had just had a call that another patient in cardiac arrest was on their way. As we had some time before divers would get down to the tug I told the ambulance service I would get someone out to the scene as soon as possible. I immediately phoned Peter Ernst and he went straight to the scene from his home.

The police divers who had the task of trying to locate the trapped men came to the department to interview the sailors who were recovering from hypothermia. Using a diagram of the tug the survivors indicated where they thought their colleagues were likely to be. At the same time, the media were arriving at the department and BBC news cameras were being set up outside the doors.

Despite two resuscitations in progress, other patients coming in, the follow-up clinic and now police divers and the media, by 11am peace was established. The department was relatively calm when members of the community health council called for a visit. "Quiet this morning then," said one member. I decided not to say anything about the morning events and leave them to watch the 6pm news! Unfortunately, no one other than the three men with hypothermia survived the disaster.

* * *

Having established myself as the nursing officer, when appointing new staff I engaged them for internal rotation, which was a new practice at Orsett. I also encouraged any day or night staff who wanted to internally rotate to do so. I introduced twilight shifts that increased staff numbers and helped relieve pressure during the evenings from 6pm-midnight and part-time staff to work in the follow-up clinic.

Today many senior nurses do not work weekends or bank holidays as it costs the employer more. However, in the 1980s, as a clinical nursing officer, I could justify working these days as, with fewer registered nurses, less support in the hospital and often decisions to be made, junior staff could find this challenging or even impossible to handle. Normally I worked a split shift on a Saturday and early shift on a Sunday.

Sunday mornings were still quiet. People either had a very lazy morning or went to church. Apart from the local corner shop, none of the large stores were open. It was usual for the receptionist to ask me to speak to people on the phone who needed advice. There was no NHS Direct or NHS 111 so A&E was the information point for a whole range of questions. One lady regularly phoned on a Sunday morning convinced she was poisoning herself. Some weeks it would be: "I'm sure I have carbon monoxide poisoning. I've a gas fire and last night the man on the TV said they poisoned you." Another Sunday: "I'm poisoned. I put two Sterident tablets in the glass with my dentures instead of one." My reply was: "That won't poison you. Rinse your dentures under a running cold tap."

Sunday afternoons were busy. Football, rugby, cricket and DIY injuries all gave us a heavy workload. Then there was the occasional elderly patient left by the relatives because they could no longer cope. Although district nurses were available, the service was limited and if it were not for us providing the district nurses with urinary catheters or specific types of wound dressings at the weekends, more patients would have come our way.

Social care at weekends was non-existent so many relatives looking after an elderly family member felt abandoned. My heart would sink when an ambulance arrived with an elderly person and no relatives. The story was always he or she had fallen from the bed or wheelchair. Almost all had no injury but with no support, relatives had given up. Classically phone calls to the relatives would not be answered and it would prove to be impossible to send the patient home. Medical on-call staff would not admit, orthopaedic medical staff would not admit and care of the elderly would argue that just because the person was old it did not mean they needed to be in the hospital. If all else failed the few beds allocated to A&E on one of the surgical wards would be used, but we all knew this would cause intense debate and criticism on Monday morning.

Ironically, during the week, we probably had one of the best social services of any A&E department. The hospital social workers were located at the end of the A&E corridor. If any of the qualified staff was concerned about an elderly person, a patient going home alone or the possibility of child abuse, we would simply walk up the corridor and put our concerns to one of the social workers. They would then take over. A similar system was in place with the community nurse liaison team. We would walk to the liaison office, explain our concerns to the liaison nurse and she would take the case on and organise community-nursing care. Teamwork was one of the great advantages of working at Orsett Hospital.

Another excellent service we received was from the coroner's officer, Bob Goddard, who was a police officer based in the hospital. Bob would initially investigate any death that would involve the coroner. All deaths that occurred in A&E would be referred to Bob, and if the relatives were present, he would either speak with them in the department or visit them when they had gone home. He always provided support to relatives especially parents of sudden infant death. It was Bob's concern for relatives that had the coroner agree to hold hospital related inquests in the hospital setting rather than in court.

Child abuse was always a matter of great concern to all involved, as was sudden infant death. For the medical and nursing staff recognition of possible abuse meant referral to social workers and the paediatric team at Basildon. For Bob it was always ensuring a sudden infant death was not connected with any abuse. One Sunday afternoon my colleague David was working on the minors' area and I was on majors. David came over to inform me of a child with scalds to his lower legs and feet who was being referred to the paediatric department. Both the doctor and David believed the child had deliberately been placed in very hot water as his feet, ankles and lower legs were scalded. The scalds stopped at exactly the same height on both legs. The parents had told the doctor and David they had found the scalds when they took the boys socks off. Now it may be that the parent ran a bath for the child and forgot to test the temperature of the water. This would not be deliberate abuse but would raise concerns about care. Their ridiculous story may have been because they realised their error, or it was an attempt to cover up abuse. Either way, their account was unbelievable and the child was at risk.

On one shift I was dealing with a very difficult father. His daughter was seriously ill and needed to be admitted to the children's unit at Basildon Hospital (Orsett had no in-patient child facilities). The father demanded that the paediatricians came to Orsett and his child was not going to Basildon. Despite discussion the father became more aggressive and sent a chair flying across the clinical room. At that point I said, "Look, I know we should have children's beds, but we don't, and neither you nor I are going to change it this afternoon. The only person suffering is your child so let me get her to Basildon." With this, the father thrust the child into my arms saying: "Take her and I'll be back in the morning." He then stormed out.

* * *

But not all Sunday afternoons were hectic and during one I heard the sound of the ice cream van and asked the staff if they would like some refreshment. The van was parked by the cricket pitch and as I reached it the man serving asked me the score. He then realised my white coat was not that of the umpire and apologised. When I told him I was from the A&E department, he asked if he could call at the department on a Sunday afternoon. I said yes, so for the rest of the summer, the van, with its chimes ringing out a tune, would arrive at the door. It was the only time of the week that patients complained if they were called to see the doctor as they wanted to finish their ice cream.

Locally we had a number of travellers' camps and two of the families were often in the department. Although there was normally only one patient, at least half of the very large family came with them. They were always polite and respectful to the staff, but the volume of people could be somewhat disruptive. Being regular visitors, I came to know the families very well. On one occasion when the department was extremely busy, and waiting times were lengthy, a patient in the waiting room started complaining and became quite abusive and threatening to one of the nurses. Before I could intervene, the male travellers surrounded the patient and nurse. "Are you all right nurse? Can we help?" It was clear they were defending the nurse, and the patient immediately sat down and not another word was heard from him.

Another time, a matriarch of the traveller's family arrived quite unwell. After examination and treatment, she needed admission to hospital. She refused, saying she would die in her caravan and not in the hospital. As many of the family knew me, they were convinced I could persuade her to stay. "She'll listen to you nurse. Tell her she has to stay in." I felt honoured they trusted me but I also felt under pressure to achieve the desired outcome. Fortunately, after a long discussion with her, including a promise that if she reached a stage where nothing else could be done she could go back to her caravan to die, she agreed to stay in the hospital, much to my relief.

* * *

The major incident plan for Orsett had not been updated for some time and I was keen to ensure the department, and the hospital, was prepared for any eventuality. As part of the Port of London major incident exercises, we would send a team to the scene and receive 'victims' from the incident. These exercises were very well planned and involved one of the major industries along the Thames. The exercise would involve a ship or ships at the refineries' landing stage, numerous casualties and normally fire and the potential for explosion. We would send a team of several doctors and nurses. In the department, the hospital would be put on major incident alert and all staff would respond as if the mock victims were real casualties.

Other such exercises included a terrorist attack on a Territorial Army unit with all injured victims coming to the department. This was such a high profile exercise the BBC sent television cameras to the hospital and we had external monitoring from London A&E managers.

Before the last section of the M25 from Potters Bar to the Thames River Crossing had opened in April 1983 another exercise involved a simulated multi-vehicle crash. With this incident, we sent a medical/nursing team to the scene and received patients in the department. Being staged at night made the whole event much more difficult yet also brought a realistic feel to the exercise. All of these exercises helped us learn lessons and improve the disaster plan.

That same section of motorway was where Peter Ernst decided to see how quickly he would be able to drive from the M11 junction (junction 27) to the A13 junction (junction 30) in an emergency. It was a Sunday morning and the BASICS doctors had been given permission to view the layout of the junctions and road system before it opened. With me as a passenger we met the other doctors and after the review, Peter shot off down the M25. The car was well in excess of the speed limit, and as I looked ahead I spotted something across the road. Hitting the brakes, Peter brought the car to a screeching halt within feet of a large metal barrier. As I sat somewhat shaken I thought to myself: we could have been the first M25 road traffic victims, even before the motorway opened.

One potential major incident event we had not planned for was an anonymous phone call stating there was a bomb in the filtration duct of the main operating theatres. Although the hospital management and police thought it was a hoax call (there had been a number of these since an IRA bomber had been discovered trying to attach a bomb to the oil tank at the local refinery), the threat was taken seriously. Although one of the four theatres had to continue as an operation was in progress the rest of the theatre suite, pharmacy, CSSD, pathology, and surrounding offices were evacuated. As A&E was directly opposite theatres, I was concerned that if there was a substantial explosion the front of A&E would be involved. I immediately evacuated the three patient rooms and offices that overlooked the theatres and directed any patients who had been seen and discharged to exit via the X-ray corridor and outpatients. Fortunately, there was no bomb, but it did make us all consider internal as well as external disaster planning.

* * *

When the Space Shuttle 'Enterprise' was piggybacked on top of a Boeing 747 into Stansted airport on 5th June 1983, I had the opportunity to work with the BASICS doctors. At that time Stansted was a very small airport mainly serving freight flights and small private planes, nothing like the airport of today. There was one country road into Stansted and traffic lights stopped cars when a plane was due to land. It was estimated that thousands of people would come to see the landing so the doctors were asked to set up medical treatment stations on the airport grounds. If any disaster occurred, or if anyone became ill or injured, medical help would be available.

I worked in one of the main medical tents and during the day, several people needed attention. As part of the medical team, I had the opportunity to go to the runway and watch the Boeing 747 land with the Space Shuttle on its back. It was amazing to see it up close.

During the afternoon, a young lady came into the tent with acute abdominal pain. The BASICS doctor (one of the GPs I knew very well) diagnosed a probable appendicitis with a degree of peritonitis. It was going to be very difficult to get her to the hospital. By this time thousands of people were at the airport and the one route out was jammed with cars either entering or leaving the airport. The doctor set up IV fluids on the lady and gave her pain killers. We were all very worried about her condition and at one point, a helicopter transfer was considered (though in 1983 such transport was not as available as it is today). Eventually, we did manage to get her out in an ambulance but it certainly proved the need for on-site medical care.

Similar on-site facilities were needed during the 400 year celebrations of Queen Elizabeth I coming to Tilbury to review her troops preparing for the Spanish invasion. In August 1588, on a field at West Tilbury, the Queen made her famous speech "I know I have the body of a weak and feeble woman, but I have the heart and stomach of a king, and of a king of England too." During the weekend of 6-7th August 1988, a great armada pageant was organised. Hearing about these plans in 1987 and the scale of the event, I contacted the organisers to ask about first aid and medical cover. It was envisaged that hundreds if not thousands of people would attend during the two days and I wanted to try to have as many injured/ill people treated on site rather than going to Orsett.

Peter Ernst was very keen to be involved, as was Don Wyatt from Essex Red Cross. Together we planned a complete emergency strategy with six first aid/emergency medical posts strategically placed along the whole route. Some 80-100 personnel on a rota system would staff these over the two-day event.

It turned out to be one of the hottest weekends in August for many years. Kate O'Mara played Elizabeth I and the event started at the Tower of London where she departed for Tilbury in the Royal Shallop (the barge that had been used in the film A Man for All Seasons). Ms O'Mara rode a white horse into Tilbury Fort where she reviewed the troops.

Many participants were in Elizabethan dress. These clothes were very thick, and by the afternoon, the temperature inside the quadrangle of the fort was intense. One by one people were collapsing with heat exhaustion. All the first aid and medical/nursing personnel were very busy rehydrating the many casualties. The pageant moved off from the fort starting the two-mile journey to the common.

As I walked the route, people were still collapsing in the heat. Going into one of the medical tents I saw a lady was fitting due to heat exhaustion. With saline fluids and tepid sponging, her temperature was controlled. When she fully recovered, she was advised to go home. "I will not give up" was her reply and, despite our advice, she donned all the thick Elizabethan clothing again as she was so determined to complete the pageant.

Kate O'Mara, resplendent on her white horse, surrounded by others on horseback and accompanied by her troops marching behind, progressed onto Parsonage Common. The festivities went on until 10.20pm. It had been a very long and busy day for all the staff and we were going to have to do it all again tomorrow.

Various activities were planned for the Sunday with the highlight being that famous speech with the 'Queen' surrounded by hundreds of her troops. As the firework display brought the weekend to a close, I breathed a sigh of relief, and was very proud of the medical, nursing and Red Cross personnel that had given up their time, and provided such a professional service to the event.

* * *

Following the Herald of Free Enterprise disaster, the emergency services tested their plans for responding to a major marine incident in Essex. The scenario was a North Sea ferry with 250 volunteers on board. It was placed five miles off-shore and then, with the use of ballast, the ferry was deliberately listed to one side. At the same time, a number of small boats full of volunteers were put into the sea just short of the ferry. I was one of the volunteers and as I sat with others looking out onto a dark, relatively calm sea, the sky was clear and the air was chilly.

At 7pm the ferry began the exercise by sending out an emergency call and sounding the ship's horn. As we sat on the boat, we could see the ferry listing and hear the call for passengers to go to their lifeboat stations. Suddenly the lights on the ferry went out and a quiet and very eerie atmosphere descended. After what felt like an eternity the silence was broken by the sound of helicopters and boats heading to the ferry. Looking up into the dark night sky the lights of the helicopters approached and, in the sea, a number of red, white and green lights were heading towards us. The idea was for the emergency services to evacuate the ferry. At the same time, our boat was taken back to the shore as we were now playing the first survivors.

As I stepped from the boat and was taken to the major incident arrival point, many of the ambulance staff and the medical team from Colchester Hospital recognised me. They were all convinced I was an observer and would be reporting on how well (or badly) they had performed. Despite assuring them I was acting as a casualty with the Red Cross they would not believe me. Even when I got to the A&E at Colchester, all the nursing staff were sure I was checking up on them.

Out of all the major incident exercises I have been involved with, that night was by far the most realistic. It was certainly very different to a 'table top' exercise in London I took part in. This involved rehearsing a major incident at Heathrow airport and how the Underground and network could be used to transport injured people to hospitals all across London and the South East.

A week before the exercise all hospitals had recorded bed availability and A&E activity at a given time on a given morning. This was the time and day that was planned for the exercise. On the table top were plastic jugs representing tube trains and paper straws representing the patients. With London Transport staff and representatives from all the emergency services and A&E units involved, we acted out the emergency response. Although quite a bizarre exercise, it did give a good indication of how patients could rapidly be moved to hospitals many miles from the airport.

* * *

During 1984, I chose to undertake the City & Guilds Further Education Teachers Certificate (FETC) at Thurrock College. The school of nursing was encouraging staff who taught and assessed student and pupil nurses in the clinical setting to undertake such training. Although funds did not stretch to all staff, the more senior members were financed to undertake the qualification. The course participants came from all professions and areas of work. There was a small number of us from the NHS; others worked for private organisations, dental practices, and industry. The tutor was a strange chap who would explain the importance of preparation and good quality teaching materials and then turn up ill-prepared and with poor overheads that had not been updated for years.

The course ended in the early summer and I was awarded the FETC with distinction in June. I had the lecturer/practice educator qualification added to my registration in August 1984 and this is still effective with the Nursing & Midwifery Council today.

I also received the 1985 RCN 3M Health Care A&E Award which was presented at the inaugural meeting of the Essex A&E group. Since 1983 the local RCN branch and AEMT committee had been running annual study days. In 1985 I encouraged A&E nurses in Essex to join and form an Essex A&E group. I was elected chair of the group and retained the position until 1995

My A&E award enabled me to research waiting times and the potential for reducing them by direct nursing intervention. It also meant I could review currently extended and advanced life support procedures practised by nurses in A&E, current nurse education within A&E and the requirements for training to enable the nurse to contribute to an improvement in the service. The study took several months with the full report being distributed during 1986. I sent copies of the report entitled 'Today and to the future' to the Department of Health and Social Security, the RCN, 3M Health Care and our district

Receiving the RCN A&E 3M Health Care Award from 3M's Peter Radcliffe in 1985   Photo: Thurrock Gazette

general manager. My work was published in the *Nursing Times/Mirror* in October 1986.

My study included visits to a number of UK hospitals. I visited Northern Ireland in November 1985 while the Troubles were still very much in the news. I arrived at Aldergrove airport, now renamed Belfast International, and took the airport bus to the city, passing through the police checkpoints on the airport road. Arriving at the Europa bus station, I decided to walk up to the Royal Victoria Hospital where Kate O'Hanlon, the A&E senior sister was expecting me. I passed the police station surrounded by a high brick wall and barbed wire and the many look out towers.

As I walked up Grosvenor Road, I could see houses burnt out and debris all over the place. Army trucks were patrolling the streets and soldiers were poised on rooftops with rifles drawn. It all felt very alien. When I arrived at the hospital, there were huge metal gates at all entrances to the site. Once inside the A&E department, I could have been in any A&E in England, except for the bulletproof glass in front of the reception desk. Staff were going about their daily tasks looking after patients with all the routine injuries and illnesses that we had at Orsett.

Having spent some time with Kate and her staff, I was told that the senior nurse of the fracture clinic, Peter O'Brien, had kindly agreed for me to use his flat in Broadway Towers. Kate, Peter and I went across to the block and while sitting chatting they advised me not to stand close to the window. The army was located on the top floors and had a lookout on the roof, so stray bullets that were intended for them could come through the window of the flat.

Soon after they left I decided to walk to a small local supermarket to buy provisions. By now, it was dark and on the way back into the towers, I heard rustling in the bushes. To my surprise, a soldier in camouflage holding a rifle confronted me. He did not say a word but watched me enter the towers and call the lift.

The next morning I crawled around the kitchen getting my breakfast trying to avoid any stray bullets. I often wondered if the warning about standing by the window was a joke but I later discovered it was all too real. In Nurses' Voices from the

Northern Ireland Troubles (published in 2013) a nurse who lived in the Towers tells the story of a bullet coming through her flat window into her pillow and then lodging in the bedroom wall.

Kate took me to visit the Mater Hospital, Belfast City Hospital, and Craigavon Hospital. As we walked to her car parked on the Falls Road she said: "Don't worry about a bomb under the car, they all know mine." Up until that point, I had not thought of bombs under cars. Now I did.

The second day I was meeting Kate in the afternoon so during the morning decided to take a walk around the local area. I walked up Broadway and onto the Falls Road which I had seen on the news and knew it was often a scene of conflict. As I walked from the hospital towards the city, the murals became more and more anti-British. There were burnt-out buildings and the road showed all the signs of past battles. I was probably half a mile from the hospital when I decided to turn around and make a hasty retreat back to the relative security of the flat.

Visiting the shopping areas of central Belfast with Kate was another 'different' experience. Designated entrances had been established around the city centre and we had to pass through a metal turnstile. All bags were searched so a simple shopping trip was a demanding experience. But I am pleased to say that my first visit to Belfast did not deter me from returning and one evening some years later, while out at a restaurant, a tone on Helen's pager indicated it was a major incident call. As senior sister of the Royal Hospital A&E she immediately went to a phone. Then just as quickly she returned asking if anyone had a

10p coin. It turned out to be a false alarm and I joked about how impressed I was that the major incident plan for Belfast relied on a 10p coin.

Today I have many friends across the Province and enjoy walking around the city and seeing how different everything is. The Falls and Shankhill roads are now even on the hop-on-hop-off tourist bus route and you see visitors from around the world photographing the now famous murals.

16 THE EIGHT MILE CORRIDOR

Major change in the NHS came in 1985 when the government accepted recommendations to take a more 'business-like' approach to the health service. Roy Griffiths, director of Sainsbury's supermarkets, was commissioned to review the management structure in the NHS. He famously said: "If Florence Nightingale were carrying her lamp through the corridors of the NHS today she would almost certainly be searching for the people in charge." So he recommended that general management should replace 'consensus' management. The RCN opposed the recommendations and produced posters indicating that Florence Nightingale would not be searching for the person in charge because she would be that person. District Health Authorities had until the end of 1985 to appoint unit general managers.

Under the new local general management structure, for the first time Orsett and Basildon hospitals became a single management unit (acute services) with one general manager (Graham Coomber). By February 1986, Graham had published his proposed management structure. The philosophy was for the two hospitals to be seen as one with an eight-mile corridor (the A13!). All key management positions, including nursing, were to cover both hospitals. There would be one director of nursing services (DNS) and one director of midwifery. The DNS would be managed and accountable to the general manager. Not since the introduction of the role of matron back in the 1800s was someone other than a nurse directly managing nurses. This move was the start of a significant shift towards non-nurse managers having a direct influence over nursing care. Under the plan, the DNS would manage nursing through four heads of nursing services: one for surgery, one for medicine, one for outpatients including day surgery and one for orthopaedics including A&E.

I argued for a head of nursing service for A&E, with the orthopaedic wards and fracture clinics becoming part of the surgery service. I believe the internal politics were such that the plan remained unchanged other than the title was now head of nursing services (orthopaedics/A&E) and a nurse specialist for A&E was to be recruited. Although the specialist post would have suited me, I could not risk working under a head of nursing service that may have very different views.

So I applied for the head of nursing services post and was successful. The new post began in July and with Brenda Lamb as director of nursing and the other heads of nursing services we met with Mr Gonzalez. His role had changed from district nursing officer to that of a professional advisor.

For me, that first meeting was not as positive as I had hoped. I suggested that my role should stay clinical as well as managerial but the idea was not welcomed. Although I spent time on the orthopaedic wards, my main concern was to bring Basildon A&E up to the same standard as Orsett. Although the nursing care was good, there was no initial assessment or triage. Also missing at Basildon was an A&E consultant. Unlike Orsett, the consultant cover at Basildon was through a nominated orthopaedic consultant who never visited, let alone worked in the department.

Although I made some simple changes that the staff had been requesting for some time, initial assessment and triage were important and I planned to introduce them as quickly as possible. It required some structural changes to the department including knocking through a wall to create a doorway and setting up a clinical area where triage could be undertaken. By the autumn, I was ready for a week off.

I chose Pontins holiday camp in Suffolk. Sir Fred Pontin donated a free week each year to the Red Cross at both his Blackpool holiday camp and the one at Pakefield near Lowestoft. Five Red Cross counties arranged for disabled people to have a holiday and Essex invited over 60 people. Each county had a coordinator, nurse, and helpers mainly from local Red Cross centres. Stan and Thelma from Grays Red Cross Centre had attended as helpers for some years and would always return full of stories of the holiday.

In 1985, the nurse at the Red Cross event had such a busy time that the coordinator insisted that the following year a second nurse should attend. I was asked if I would volunteer and I jumped at the chance. Arriving before the guests gave me the opportunity to see the area of the holiday camp that Essex occupied. We were very lucky as our chalets were in a square with surrounding gardens. Some were designated for helpers such as I and one chalet was the surgery. Before the guests arrived we organised ramps made by the camp carpenters for those in wheelchairs and ensured all chalets were ready for the guests. Stan had a list of all guests who required raised beds; this was achieved by using bricks from the camp. Other alterations included toilet doors being removed for wheelchair users.

All guests were allocated a team with a team leader and helpers. The two nurses provided care for all the guests. As the coaches arrived we helped move the guests to their chalets. Once there, the team leader welcomed them and checked their personal needs such as mobility and bathing. Rosina was the other nurse. She made it clear in her opening remarks to me that she was the boss and I was her assistant. Even though I was a head of nursing services at work, I happily accepted this role. Rosina was a retired gynaecological ward sister and it was clear she ran the nursing at Pontins as she had probably run her ward.

I was instructed to take half the chalets and establish nursing needs such as wound dressing and medication. I would then report to Rosina. Once everything was sorted guests went to the dining room for afternoon tea. Later it was dinner and then over to the ballroom for the evening entertainment. All guests who needed assistance had a group of helpers allocated.

During the early evening of that first day, one of the guests became unwell. After taking him back to the chalet, I could see the man was having difficulty breathing, his skin was blue and he was complaining of chest pain. Rosina arrived and was clearly as concerned as I was. We called an ambulance. If an emergency arose anywhere on the camp, the Red Cross ambulance crew would respond. A senior Red Cross ambulance officer (who was by profession a full-time county ambulance attendant/driver) coordinated these volunteers. By now, I knew the man required oxygen and although no emergency cylinder was available, one of the other guests had oxygen in his chalet so I brought the cylinder to the scene. I was now well into my normal role as an A&E nurse. When the ambulance crew arrived, I explained the situation and continued to take the lead on the way to hospital.

Following that incident Rosina's attitude towards me changed. She complemented me on the way I had handled the emergency and recognised my ability as an emergency nurse. From that moment, our working relationship improved dramatically although I always treated her as the boss.

After the events of my first 'holiday' the next year I took more equipment, including a portable manual defibrillator. Because of my speciality the ambulance co-ordinator and the camp organiser asked if I would provide emergency care for the camp when an incident was more complex than the ambulance crew could deal with. I was happy to do this and to continue my main role as a nurse to the Essex guests.

One responsibility was to provide emergency cover for the boat ride on The Broads. Every day the guests had various outings and on a Wednesday afternoon, it was the boat ride. Two craft were hired and several coaches of guests were transported to Wroxham. On arrival, it was a case of helping people from the coach onto the boats. Wheelchairs were the most difficult as shingle paths were hard to negotiate and as the boats were not designed for wheelchairs we would have to lift the chair and guest and literally drop them into the boat. Getting them out was even more difficult but every guest despite their disability enjoyed the day.

I also made myself available on the boats should an emergency arise. I was stationed on one boat with my equipment and the plan was that if an emergency occurred on the other boat a hooter would sound, the two boats would come together and I would leap from one to the other. Fortunately, I never had to test out this plan.

With a number of guests in each boat and only one toilet, it meant that anyone in a wheelchair had very little chance of using it. One afternoon one of our young female wheelchair guests said she needed the toilet. It was going to be impossible to get her into the boat toilet and, as we were near to docking, I asked her if she could hold on and I would ensure we got her off first. Having done that I then rushed around pushing the wheelchair and trying to find a public toilet. The only one open was on a remote part of the marina and, as I got the wheelchair in, it was clear the cubicle doorway was too narrow. By this time the young lady was in great distress so I gave the chair one almighty push and this forced the cubicle door off of its hinges. Having achieved our goal, to the young lady's relief, we then left the toilet, both agreeing not to say a word about the cubicle door.

One year I was woken by the night staff asking if I could go down to a chalet in the Norfolk area of the camp where I found one of the ambulance crew with a guest in agonising pain. He had a catheter in situ attached to a night drainage bag. There was no urine in the bag and the guest had a full bladder. I was asked: "Can you unblock the catheter?" As I disconnected the bag urine poured out. I removed the protective cover from the connection on the drainage bag and reconnected the two. All was sorted.

The helpers and ambulance crew were very embarrassed. "Don't be," I said. "I only knew that was a probability because I have seen the cover left on so many times in the hospital."

Although the ambulance crew was available to deal with emergencies, if someone was just feeling unwell, one of the local GPs would visit. This happened one evening with a guest who had great difficulty with speech and was very deaf. We called the GP who was also very deaf and it played out like a sketch from Monty Python. The GP would ask a question and the guest would reply: "What did you say?" Then the GP, not hearing the reply, asked what the guest had said. To make matters worse, the guest had an artificial heart valve (one of the ball and cage type) so the more he became agitated the more the ticking sound in his chest increased in speed and frequency.

On another occasion one of our guests was complaining of severe pain from his leg stump. The man was a double-amputee and that night he was screaming in pain. When I arrived, the helpers were trying to keep him calm and make him comfortable on the bed. The first thing I asked was: "Is this pain something you've had before?" "Yes," he replied "And when I get it I hit the stump on the wall. These helpers won't let me do that." I told them to let him hit the stump on the wall. The pain was resolved and we could all go back to bed.

Epileptic fits were relatively common though most guests had them controlled. However, one person was continually having fits sometimes several times in an evening. It was looking as though he may end up in hospital but then we realised nearly all the fits occurred when he was in the ballroom. I looked around for a trigger and spotted the glittering ceiling rotating glass ball. Following my request to have the glass ball turned off, the fits stopped.

Pontins Pakefield holidays were an outstanding success, and for many guests this was a week away from their routine of sitting in a house or flat with very little stimulus. As the years went by, Pontins changed owners and charges for the week were introduced. Despite the Red Cross subsidising the holidays, it was becoming harder for individuals to afford the holiday and numbers dwindled. At the same time, the Red Cross undertook a major review and decided to scrap the holidays. They did not fit with the new Red Cross strategy and it was felt that the chalets did not meet the standard now expected for disabled access. Bricks to increase the height of a bed and removal of toilet doors were no longer acceptable solutions. I continued to attend every year until the final holiday in 1998.

17 ONE A&E HAS TO CLOSE

Each head of nursing services had been issued with a pager and we would work an on-call rota for the hospitals at night and weekends. I decided that if there was an A&E problem, now I had a pager I would have the staff call me rather than the on-call person. This was a decision I would come to regret after a few years in the job.

Being on-call was not an onerous task as there were always senior nurses in both hospitals to deal with day-to-day issues. We were often called if there were staffing or bed management problems or something out of the ordinary occurred. Once I was called to deal with a porter who had mental health issues and had set fire to the basement of Orsett Hospital. Another call involved a hospital manager seeking my advice over whether to call the police as a patient was passing condoms full of white powder into a bedpan. Both incidents were easily resolved with the intervention of the police.

A more bizarre event was when I was asked to go down to the stores at Basildon Hospital. The police had arrested one of the hospital doctors, charging him with attempted murder of his wife. Items were found in a lock-up he owned and I was told several of them had A&E stamped on the packaging. The police said they were returning them but when I arrived in the hospital stores, I could not believe my eyes. There in front of me, covering a large area of floor space, was a mass of equipment and packages. I immediately recognised our suture packs. I had been blaming the sterile supply department for weeks assuming they had lost them or not replaced them. As I went through the mound, there were dozens of stethoscopes and other examination equipment including full surgical trays from the operating theatres. One tray was for a major abdominal operation, another for a caesarean section. Some equipment and surgical trays were from as far away as Liverpool while others were from wards and departments at Basildon and Orsett.

* * *

As the summer of 1987 arrived, dark clouds hung over our A&E departments as the fate of one department hung in the balance. The district health authority was in financial crisis and was looking to save £600,000 a year. One of the many draft plans was the closure of one of the two A&E departments. Views varied as to which should go and I thought the management would shut Orsett. To my surprise, the general manager (Graham Coomber) considered Basildon A&E to be the better option for closure and 48 beds would go at Orsett.

While preparing Orsett to become the main department I could not spend any money so no redevelopment could occur - we just had to make the current structure cope with double the numbers of patients. The local MPs and media started a campaign to reverse the closure decision and over the next couple of months, major public meetings were held.

By September, it looked certain that the closure was going ahead. Peter Ernst had arranged the doctor's rota and I had sorted the nursing rotas. However, one final push from the Basildon MP to the government meant that, with less than 48 hours to go, the Secretary of State reversed the decision. I received a phone call telling me I had to ensure that Basildon remained open. It was a nightmare, with staff rotas having to be redrawn and I had to engage agency nurses to fill the gaps where some Basildon staff had left. Then we had to return the offices at Orsett that we had converted to clinical rooms back to their original purpose. Still, the long-term fate of Basildon lay in the balance; uncertainty was still going to overshadow everything until the end of the year when it was finally agreed the unit would remain open.

Since being appointed head of nursing services for orthopaedics/ A&E I had been keen to move orthopaedics to surgery and regain A&E as a stand-alone service. Negotiating the removal of the orthopaedic wards was less traumatic than I expected. I first discussed the idea with Lydia (head of nursing surgery) and she agreed. Next I won over Brenda (director of nursing) and Graham Coomber (acute unit general manager). The final move was Lydia and I setting up a meeting with the consultants to explain why it would be better for the wards to be part of the overall surgical division. They agreed, so for me it was a case of 'goodbye orthopaedics!'

* * *

The need to improve nursing documentation was often a topic at Brenda's weekly meetings and it was the right time to consider a computerised system linked with a model of nursing. I agreed that any model used in A&E had to link with the wards but could not contain all the same elements, as the ward would require far more in-depth care planning. It was agreed that, working together, a model for A&E could be designed that would then link into a more detailed model on the ward. Over several months, an A&E model was developed and by using a practice-based system of design, we eventually achieved our goal. I named the A&E model the Components of Life model.

From this, Sister Lesley Green and Pat McKeogh developed a dependency tool that ensured every patient had a dependency score allocated on arrival in the A&E department and this was subsequently updated throughout their stay. The dependency tool used the same key headings as the Components of Life model and enabled a clearer link between patient dependency and staff allocation, and provided a clear picture of the overall workload in the department.

Linking the model and dependency scoring to a computer and then linking it with the ward system was some time away. However, I was so pleased with the way the staff in both departments had worked with me on the project. I wanted to publish our work so I started writing my second book and signed the contract in July 1989 with Faber & Faber. It was called Accident & Emergency Nursing - A Structured Approach and was published in 1990. Through my profile with the RCN A&E Association, articles/books I had written, and interviews on the national news, the developments at Orsett and Basildon were becoming well known, and nurse managers from other areas came to visit.

Although I had negligible clinical time, I really enjoyed the evenings I worked at Orsett. I was back in my comfort zone and felt as though I had never been away from the white coat, keys in my pocket and caring for patients. I would often agree to run the department so that the staff could go out socially. This gave me a real opportunity to ensure everything was how I wanted. I also did some night clinical work usually between midnight and 4am. The pace had certainly changed since my nights in 1975, particularly at Basildon. The patients were coming in throughout the early hours reflecting the social change with more nightclubs opening and working hours changing. This caused me to increase the number of nurses working at night.

In addition to my infrequent evening shifts, I occasionally would be asked for my clinical input, especially if a male patient had an 'embarrassing' problem. Throughout my clinical life, I have always believed in affording patients as much dignity as possible. In A&E, I would always try to have a female nurse assess a patient with any gynaecological condition and, if available, a male nurse for male patients with any condition or injury to the genitalia. The foreskin of the penis trapped in a trouser zip was common and although easily sorted it always caused embarrassment to the man. More unusual was the occasion a man arrived with a vibrator in his rectum. The device was still active and illuminated and had become trapped far higher up in the bowel than was the intention when it was introduced. Despite various attempts, we could not retrieve it, but it was very interesting to look at the X-ray and see its inner workings. Eventually the man had it removed in the operating theatre under general anaesthetic.

I was glad I was available at Orsett A&E when a call came through for the mobile accident team to attend a multi-vehicle pile-up on the M25. Without hesitation, and before anyone else had a chance, I said I would go. The SHO and one of the enrolled nurses (Sharon) who had never been out with the team accompanied me. We changed into our protective clothing and once the ambulance arrived, we were off. The incident was on the M25 just north of the A13 junction. A man was trapped in the cab of his lorry and another trapped in a car.

I suggested to the doctor and Sharon that they attend to the man in the car while I climbed up to the lorry driver. The ambulance crew and a passing doctor were already attending to him. The doctor had started an IV infusion and the driver was relatively stable. I then went to the car and found Sharon with the ambulance crew. I asked where the doctor was and was told "In the ambulance." I stepped in and asked the doctor why she was not with the patient. "I'm waiting for the fire crew to get him out of the car so that I can treat him," she said. I explained to her that the idea was she treats him in the car. "If you wait till they get him out, he will be dead. Please go and get IV fluids into him so he has a chance." Once the two men were free, they were transported to Orsett. I was so pleased to be back in the thick of it but knew my future role was to be elsewhere doing something different.

* * *

The business ethos was really starting to take hold in the NHS with requests (or demands) from managers for ideas to generate income. One such idea was to charge visitors to park in the hospital car park. I was appalled. My view was that patients and relatives did not want to come to the hospital - it was a necessity. To charge them for parking seemed totally against what caring was all about. Despite many other staff feeling the same way, our views were ignored and parking charges were introduced.

Another brainwave was to put numerous vending machines in all waiting areas. A&E had always had a simple drinks machine and even that often caused a mess. But management's view was 'more machines - more income'. When the hospital administrator suggested a chip-frying machine in the waiting room, I could hardly believe it. Despite my protests, pressure from more senior managers was brought to bear. So, to show them how stupid the idea was, I agreed for a trial in one A&E. Basildon got the machine but it lasted less than a week. Every time it operated the whole department smelt like a fish and chip shop. The orthopaedic consultant complained he could smell it in the fracture clinic and staff in adjoining departments were unhappy too. I took great delight seeing it go.

One of the biggest challenges during this period was a new structure for nurses' pay. Called clinical grading it involved staff being banded into one of several pay bands. It was left to individual hospitals to decide how each nurse fitted into a particular band. The A&E nurse managers in what was then North East Thames Regional Health Authority had foreseen the problems that were about to occur throughout the country. So as a body, we agreed that we would offer the same grades in our A&E departments, thus removing the prospect of one department being played off against the others. We also felt that standing together we would be able to prevent our staff being graded at a lower band than we thought appropriate. I succeeded in awarding the grades that reflected the individuals' responsibilities and none of my staff appealed. This collaboration led to the establishment of an informal regional A&E nurse managers group, which I chaired. We met on a regular basis, our purpose being the improvement of A&E services across the region. Although not a formal group within the regional structure, the regional office did support us and one of the regional nurses (Kate Harmond) attended the meetings.

It was good that I had the RCN A&E Forum as an outlet to discuss all that was happening in the NHS. As the public relations officer of the forum, I worked with the other honorary officers and was able to travel all around the country meeting members and setting up new local forums. Within two years, nine new local forums were established, making 16 forums across the UK and some 3,000 members (a doubling of the membership in two years). Being keen to link the A&E forum with regional RCN activities, I proposed that I be allowed to sit on the regional committee as a link between local and national A&E activity. This was agreed and I represented the A&E forum until I became an RCN Council member in 1995. In recognition of my work at regional and national level, the members of the committee presented me with the annual North East Thames Regional Merit Award 1994.

With the other national forum officers, I attended RCN Congress and took advantage of presenting resolutions that would benefit patients in A&E. The hotel for our second congress, in Glasgow, was linked to the main railway station and was clearly the hotel used by local prostitutes. In fact, the whole area was a red light district. One evening, looking for the main conference venue, we realised we were lost. To the surprise of my colleagues, I walked over to one of the prostitutes and asked her where the hotel was. She said she would take me! I thanked her for the kind offer but indicated I was with friends and just needed directions, to which she obliged.

Throughout my period as chair of the A&E association from 1987-1995 I continued to tour the UK speaking at local study days and conferences. It was in 1989, for the first time, I stood up in front of an international audience in Hong Kong and

As chair of the RCN A&E Association I spoke at many international events

presented a clinical paper. In fact, I presented two, one on hydrofluoric acid burns and the second on pre-hospital care in the UK. This conference was the first of many international events where I presented papers, including Singapore, Australia and in several American states including Hawaii.

I was on crutches when I attended the 1990 RCN Congress following an accident at work. I had fractured my heel bone when I fell from a worksurface I should not have been standing on (even A&E nurses can ignore health and safety!). At that year's congress as I stood at the microphone and introduced myself: "Gary Jones, Chair, Accident & Emergency Association." The hall erupted with laughter. It took a few seconds for me to get the joke - here I was, the A&E leading light, hobbling around on crutches. People still tease me about that over 30 years later.

18 THE END OF AN ERA

The predicaments of the NHS today can be traced back to the late 1980s. Although the introduction of general management could be seen as the start of the commercialisation of the NHS, it was in January 1989 when it really began to accelerate. The government was proposing changes to the NHS that would enable hospitals to have more financial autonomy under a new structure in which they would be called hospital trusts. By February, a White Paper had been published and locally staff meetings of senior managers were taking place.

The closed beds at Orsett were to remain closed and some services, such as porters and domestic staff, were to be moved out of the NHS altogether. Although many of the staff previously employed by the district transferred to the new private firms, it was not long before those staff started to leave and others came in. At the same time, it appeared as though the new firms were all about making money so staff numbers were cut and rather than the cleaners and porters being allocated a specific area of work, they were often moved from ward to ward.

In some areas of the country, although not at Orsett or Basildon, health authorities were threatening to evict nurses from NHS accommodation, a challenge the RCN was prepared to fight with legal action. In years to come, nurses, like many other staff, were no longer allocated any on-site accommodation.

The population of Thurrock was rising, mainly due to a major housing development Chafford Hundred. This, plus other factors, meant an increasing workload for local health staff. With the reduced bed numbers at Orsett, and the government pushing for a general reduction in beds across the NHS, ward occupancy was hitting 100%. When the hospital manager suggested some patients could stay overnight in A&E or the fracture clinic, I immediately dismissed the suggestion. I pointed out that A&E was not, and must never become, a holding area for patients who should be on a ward. I had seen so much of that in the US and Canada during my tour in 1980 and I was determined never to see it at Orsett or Basildon.

By October 1989, the district was on course for a deficit of £1m-£1.5m and the report to the health authority in December indicated the need for many more cuts to services. In mid-January 1990, the Basildon & Thurrock Health Authority was presented with radical proposals to centralise a number of services on one site including A&E, ITU, medicine and emergency surgery. Although the public was unaware of it, planning was moving fast. Peter Ernst was totally opposed to any suggestion of closing Orsett and he made it clear that he would do anything in his power to stop it.

At this early stage, I drew up a paper presenting the pros and cons for centralisation and put forward arguments for and against retaining both departments. Personally, I was unsure about centralisation, but if it was to happen, I wanted Orsett to survive. Yet in my heart, I knew it was a lost cause. The consultant body, Sue Jennings (the new acute services general manager) and many others in the organisation could only see one way forward and that favoured Basildon. The regional A&E

consultant body had been approached to give an independent view as to which A&E should be developed and which one should close.

Although I was off sick (as a result of the heel fracture) I was determined to be present when the consultants came to visit the departments. I arranged for a wheelchair to be available at Orsett, which is an experience all health care staff should try. As I sat in the wheelchair, the consultants and managers talked over my head, on many occasions just ignoring me and as they went from room to room they left me in the corridor. Halfway through the visit I stood up, used my crutches, abandoned the wheelchair and said: "Now can I join in?" Red faces all round, the visit continued and then we went over to Basildon.

As the visiting consultants toured the A&E at Basildon Sue Jennings pointed out the three theatres and explained how they could be utilised in an internal rebuild. She also showed them the ward that could become an A&E observation ward. Seeing these areas, plus the two large resuscitation rooms, there was little doubt that they would favour Basildon. When their report arrived, sure enough they did.

However, very soon things began to unravel. Just before Easter 1990 and my holiday to Ireland, the hospital manager at Basildon phoned me at home. He said: "Just to make you aware, following a centralisation meeting, it's been decided the ward that was to become part of A & E is now going to be a gynaecology ward. And two of the theatres are becoming endoscopy." What this meant, in reality, was that although the department was going to have a major revamp, and the one theatre that we already used would be redesigned to accommodate additional stretcher trolleys, we were now losing a substantial part of what was originally promised. I was very disillusioned and angry and wondered how many other promises would be broken as the year progressed.

By March the 'secret scheme,' as the local paper called it, was out in the public domain and anger in Thurrock was growing. During the many meetings with the public and with staff over the £750,000 centralisation plan, the managers reassured everyone that Orsett would remain a viable hospital with in-patient beds and many other services. All three MPs (two Conservative and one Labour) opposed the plans, as did Thurrock Council. Peter Ernst came out strongly against the centralisation and especially the closure of Orsett A&E. He took on the management both internally and through the local press and in doing so he became, in the eyes of the management, Enemy Number One.

I certainly did not want to fall out with Peter, but at the same time I was concerned that if I did not work with Sue Jennings and the district management the result could be someone else put in charge of the A&E centralisation planning. The district health authority approved the plans in April and despite huge public opposition (a 25,000 signature petition), and a debate on the closure in the House of Commons, with requests for the Prime Minister to intervene, by July the regional health authority had approved the plans. On 22nd September 1990, the Secretary of State for Health agreed. The fight was over, the district managers had won and Orsett A&E was lost.

I was involved from day one with the design of the new department at Basildon. I consulted the staff and encouraged them to put forward ideas as to how the department might look and what facilities we required. I spent time walking around the department to try to get the patient flow right but I regret not sticking to my guns over the need for a patient-to-doctor system for patients with minor injuries. Apart from designs and business plans for the new department, I was asked to predict the nurse staffing and skill mix. It was made clear that whatever I came up with had to save money on nursing staff costs. I decided to present a short-term staffing plan and a long-term plan. Another scheme I hatched was to try to get the porters' budget (currently paid to a private firm) into the nursing budget and create what I called 'departmental assistants'. I was successful, so when the centralised department opened I had a new grade within the nursing structure.

With the decision to centralise services at Basildon agreed, I was having difficulty recruiting nursing staff to Orsett, and some nurses were already beginning to leave. Because of this, the decision was taken to close Orsett A&E at night. On 24th September 1990, the doors swung shut at 9pm. I felt I was part of the destruction of a department I had been connected to since 1975, and it hurt. Morale was very low and it was difficult to know what I could do to improve it. Despite my positive approach to the new department, no one was that interested. I was trying very hard to show enthusiasm for what could be a better future for A&E services.

As a relief from all that was going on at Orsett and Basildon, I was glad to get the chance to travel to Chicago. Our RCN A&E Association, through the efforts of our vice-chair Ethel Buckles, was linking with the US Emergency Nurses Association (ENA) to provide an international trauma course (TNCC) in the UK. Eight UK nurses undertook the course, passing out as TNCC instructors and I signed an agreement on behalf of the A&E Association with the chief executive of the Emergency Nurses Association. In 2020 we will celebrate 30 years of providing the trauma nursing course throughout the UK and Eire.

The first phase of the building work at Basildon was to convert the theatre area into clinical facilities. Although the noise was almost intolerable, the main department continued to function. Once the builders had gone for the day, I would climb over the rubble and have a good look around. It was lucky that I did because at one point during the works I noticed a doorway established immediately behind a pillar. There was no way a stretcher trolley could be pushed in or out. The next morning the builders bricked up the doorway and sited another one in a better spot.

As 1991 progressed, the heads of nursing services and other managers were invited to attend some of the exploratory meetings around the development of trust directorates. As suspected, the focus was on medical consultants becoming clinical directors, though I did privately suggest to Sue Jennings that clinical directors could come from nursing as well as from medicine. But this was clearly not on her radar.

By late spring, the first phase of the building works at Basildon was complete. On the weekend of 25th/26th May, we moved the department into the new area and building works commenced in the main department.

I wanted to achieve a larger open spaced resuscitation room by bringing the two current rooms into one. However, we needed the ability to shut off one area from the rest of the room so it could be isolated for chemical or other hazardous incidents. There would be an external door directly into that part of the room. Most A&E departments in the early 1990s were not designed to deal with chemical or radiation contamination. In fact, the NHS did not plan as well as we do today, so my ideas for a whole trolley bay that could be isolated with an external

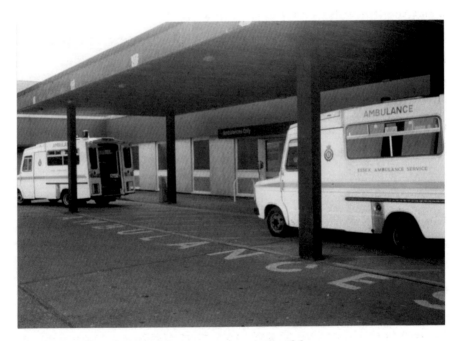

The centralised A&E Department at Basildon

door, while hardly radical, was viewed with scepticism. Nevertheless I got my way.

What I did not achieve was a helicopter-landing pad outside the department. It was early days for helicopters in day-to-day use in the health service. Even the well known Royal London Hospital helicopter had only been responding to primary calls since May 1989 and from the helipad at the hospital in Whitechapel since August 1990. When the rejection to my request came through it was because: "helicopters will not become commonplace for transporting patients in the UK" and "it would not be right to cut down the nice trees."

The work had to move very fast as the district managers had now set the centralisation date as Monday 22nd July 1991. Due to the need to keep costs as low as possible very little new equipment was to be purchased. I was told as much of the current equipment and stretcher trolleys at Orsett and Basildon were to be used. I knew this would cause even more unhappiness at Orsett as I had to start cannibalising the department of all but essential equipment and moving it over to Basildon.

Before I knew it, July was upon us and it became extremely busy. The building works for the main department at Basildon were complete. So it was now a case of preparing it for centralisation. Normally when A&E departments move, or are centralised, there is a period of closure to allow the transfer of equipment and a controlled period of preparation. Politically this could not happen with this move so a removal firm was hired to transfer the stretcher trolleys and other large items over to Basildon on the

Monday morning. I just hoped I would have enough equipment to deal with the increased patient numbers until they arrived.

When Sunday 21st July came, I felt a sense of relief that the new department was almost ready, but a greater sense of anxiety. Would it work? Would all the plans and promises come to fruition? That afternoon I went over to Orsett. There was going to be a closure party in the department that evening. It was possible to have the event in areas where no one could see or hear from outside. The last thing we needed was the public hearing a party on the final day Orsett would have an A&E department.

That afternoon is seared in my memory as if it were yesterday. I stood in the accident room with one of the enrolled nurses, Jill Fairweather, and told her I wanted something from the department as a keepsake. But it needed to be small, and truly reflect that marvellous department. But I couldn't think what it could be. Jill took a universal specimen pot and, having removed the lid, she waved it about in the air. Putting the top back on she said: "This is Orsett atmosphere." She labelled the pot 'Orsett atmosphere, date 21/7/91 time15.10'. I still have that pot today and have never opened it because Orsett A&E, and all that it meant to me, and so many other people, is still in that pot.

At 9pm that evening, Peter Ernst ceremonially locked the A&E doors for the last time. My emotions were running high, as was true for everyone else. A part of me felt angry that the staff could not see the potential for the new department. I was sad that Peter was not coming. I also felt angry with myself for not saving

Orsett, though there was little I could have done. The party was more of a wake and I was glad when it was over.

Monday 22nd July 1991 was day one for the centralised department at Basildon. I had anticipated it would take at least until mid or late afternoon to get the main department ready to open. What I had not anticipated was others wanting us to move out of the ward (our temporary waiting room) immediately so gynaecology could move in. With the large volume of patients now descending on the department, I had no choice but to open the main department before it was ready. Was this an omen for the future?

A few days before centralisation I was told that the Local MP for Basildon had negotiated with Buckingham Palace for the department to be opened by 'a Royal'. I assumed this would be several weeks in the future and after we were settled in. How wrong I was. In the week we moved in, I was informed the ceremony would be that coming Friday and 'the Royal' would be the Duke of Kent.

On Friday morning, I arrived early and police were already checking the department using dogs. At last all was ready and at 10am the Duke arrived. Just beforehand, a seriously injured man was rushed into the resuscitation room. Martin Hunt (the new A&E consultant) was required to attend to the man, so it was left to me to escort the Duke.

As the tour party moved through the department, I introduced the Duke to as many staff as possible. We stopped at the

I still have the printout with 'Aftercare instructions for Duke of Kent'

The royal opening took place the week we moved in

Photo: Basildon Hospital

computer and printer which had come over from Orsett and were being used to produce the discharge aftercare instructions. During a conference in the US in 1990, I had visited a trade stand that was exhibiting a computerised discharge planning system for A&E called Logicare. I knew this would link to the work that enrolled nurse Sally McCornack was doing through her 3M/A&E award on discharge planning at Orsett. The creator of this system was keen to link into the UK market so he had flown over to Orsett in 1991 and worked with Sally on developing a UK version. Sally spent weeks converting the US discharge information sheets into a UK version and Orsett was the first A&E in the country to use it.

I demonstrated the system to the Duke by printing a discharge aftercare instruction. He showed real interest and laughed when out of the printer came: 'Aftercare instructions for Duke of Kent Friday, July 26, 1991, 10.43am'. I still have that printout.

Many hospital managers and local dignitaries were in the waiting room as the Duke unveiled the plaque. As they left I felt pleased everything had gone well. Below the plaque we placed another stating that the new department was an amalgamation of Orsett and Basildon A&E departments. It was my way of keeping Orsett A&E alive in the new centralised department.

19 TIME TO LEAVE

When the secretary of state signed off the plans for A&E centralisation, it was stated that a minor injuries unit must open in Thurrock. Once centralisation had taken place the senior managers conveniently forgot about this plan; that was until a letter arrived from the health minister, Stephen Dorrell, indicating that he looked forward to visiting the unit and the new A&E department towards the end of the year.

Suddenly a rush was on. Sue Jennings did not want a minor injury unit under the acute sector and argued it should be community-led. The community services agreed, but Patrick Geoghegan, now community unit manager, would only take it on if I would set it up and manage it on behalf of the community services. I agreed as did Sue and Brenda Lamb (DNS). The first task was to identify a venue for the unit and I felt strongly that it should be located in the community and not in the hospital. A room in a bungalow used by the health visitors was identified in Purfleet which certainly fitted the criteria of locating it in a deprived area of the borough!

The next task was staffing it. I identified three staff nurses from A&E who were keen to take on this new venture. A very rapidly devised training programme was put together and between the A&E consultant Martin Hunt and myself, we established the first minor injury emergency nurse practitioners in our district. Protocols, policies, guidelines and much more were all pulled together within the short time frame. The three staff nurses worked away in the bungalow making it fit for its purpose.

Leaflets were printed for distribution to the public and signage to the unit established on lamp-posts in the area. Patrick (community unit manager) was very enthusiastic and I received total support from him. On 7th October 1991, the unit opened to patients and a week later Tim Janman MP for Thurrock, officially opened the unit. In December Stephen Dorrell, health minister, made his visit to both the minor injury unit and the A&E department at Basildon. I wrote an article for Nursing Standard on how the new initiative had been achieved.

Although the centralised A&E department worked well initially, by early September the number of patients attending the department was far exceeding what had been anticipated. Due to the reduced number of hospital beds it was becoming increasingly difficult to get patients onto a ward. Although Orsett should have continued to provide all non-emergency surgery, because there was no ITU, many of the anaesthetists and surgeons refused to perform major surgery there. It was becoming clear that Orsett was not going to be used as planned, and while its beds lay empty, Basildon was full to bursting. At the same time, the promised immediate availability of doctors from the specialities was not happening. By Christmas, I was wishing I did not have a pager. Even on Boxing Day, when I was out with my family for a meal, the darn thing went off. When I called the department, it was to hear the same old story that waiting times were long and no beds were available in the hospital.

At the beginning of 1992, five months into centralisation, I decided to meet all the A&E problems head on. I had several meetings with Amanda (the new director of nursing and midwifery), Sue Jennings (chief executive) and the clinical director. But I felt my message was falling on deaf ears. Despite my efforts, there appeared to be little support, and the impression given was that everything was A&E's fault. In reality, patients were not getting to the wards because of reduced bed capacity, which was a hospital issue. A&E patients were not being seen quickly, a medical staffing issue. Patients were receiving good medical and nursing care, an A&E success. All the complaints I received (and there were many) were about waiting times and not about care received. All that was happening in our A&E was a reflection of the negative picture I had witnessed in some emergency departments in Canada and the US. I had seen patients waiting hours, if not days, for a hospital bed. I had seen violence to staff, often due to frustration with the system, and hospitals focussed on profit, putting business needs before service. This was now happening in my department, and I did not like it at all.

Under the new pre-trust directorate structure, A&E became part of the directorate of orthopaedics, A&E and ENT. For A&E the sub-director was Martin Hunt, so from just Peter and I managing A&E at Orsett, we now had a director, sub-director, business manager plus myself. I had been promoted to A&E services manager so was now managing all the staff, other than the doctors, and was responsible for the business of the department. This promotion gave me the opportunity to attend a business management course. I was no longer managerially accountable to the director of nursing but was professionally accountable to her for A&E nursing services. At the same time, I was now managerially accountable to Martin and ultimately the clinical director, both medical consultants.

Regular meetings were held to continue the new directorate structure in preparation for trust status and every manager had to write a three-year business plan. The finance department was starting to structure the hospital finances into directorates which in my view was a complete disaster and led to many additional meetings. I was particularly annoyed because the finance department had taken my long-term financial plan for nurse staffing and produced it as the current finance for the department. This meant less money and statements showing a massive overspend.

Despite local opposition, particularly from Labour councillors, trust status was approved to go ahead on 1st April 1992. One of the key criteria had been a healthy financial position. Everything appeared to focus on getting the books to balance. The number of finance staff was growing as the nursing staff diminished.

A further focus on finance was reflected in the way nurses were paid for any overtime. It was my practice to pay them the rate based on their grade. Therefore, if a sister worked extra hours I paid her at a sister's rate. But this was to stop, and everyone was to be paid a single bank rate. This culture, focussing on finance, increased the sense of worthlessness some staff were now feeling. During one of our many meetings, the director of finance stated: "No one is as important as the trust." For me, that summed up the direction we were heading.

For some months, the regional A&E nurse managers had been working with Kate Harmond (regional nurse) to develop a regional guide to good practice for A&E departments. The working group was much larger than the nurse managers' group and had included representatives from the police, ambulance service, medical consultants, GPs, the regional emergency planning officer, an architect and a priest from a homeless centre.

At one meeting, I was rather subdued and because of all the issues with A&E I could not summon my usual enthusiasm. At the end of the meeting, Kate approached me and asked what was wrong. At first, I was reluctant to say but on further questioning, I told her how I felt. Her response was: "You've grown out of that job. You need something new."

That discussion got me thinking and when I contacted her shortly after the meeting, she suggested I might be interested in working at region for a six months period. Kate's idea was for me to have a short-term contract to pull together the regional A&E guidelines. Further discussions and many weeks of thinking long and hard helped me make the decision to leave Basildon and take up the six month contract.

As I had to give three months' notice, I wrote my letter of resignation in March so that my last day would be 31st May. I received some pleasant letters including one from the clinical director who said he wished to place on record his appreciation and admiration for the work that I had put into the A&E departments. The chief executive Sue Jennings wrote that it was with some sadness that she acknowledged my resignation, indicating I had contributed significantly to the improvement of standards and services in the unit. 'You will be a hard act to follow' were her closing remarks.

On a brighter note, the RCN A&E committee had been having discussions with the editor of Nursing Standard to have our newsletter upgraded to an insert into the journal. In March 1992, a 16 - page supplement appeared in Nursing Standard entitled Emergency Nurse - The journal of the RCN Accident & Emergency Nursing Association. We certainly felt we had arrived!

During the last three months at Basildon, I continued to push for improved staffing and patient flow. Before I left, it was agreed that an independent review of nurse staffing would be undertaken. I met with the nurse consultant but I had left before the report was presented to the trust. In April Basildon & Orsett hospitals, including St Andrews Hospital Billericay, became a trust. A very impressive carpet with the new trust logo was laid at the main hospital reception and all old stationary was binned.

On the 14th May, just over two weeks before my last working day, I had a phone call from Kate Harmond at region. She said that because of financial constraints she was unable to employ me for the six months work but could pay me as a self-employed consultant. I had no idea what that entailed or where to get advice. Liz Purdy (one of the minor injury nurse practitioners) suggested meeting her husband Clive who was an accountant and he explained how self-employment worked and showed me the paperwork I needed to complete. I asked him if he would become my accountant and he agreed. I signed the relevant papers and he said: "You are self-employed from 1st June." We toasted the event with a glass of lager.

My last duty day was Friday 29th May. There was a small farewell party in the department as I did not want a formal trust send off. I had a meal with friends and colleagues that evening. My plan, from the day I had decided to leave, was to undertake the six months work for the region and then look for a senior clinical A&E nursing post elsewhere. However, fate had other ideas and, though I didn't know it at the time, Sunday 31st May 1992 was to be the last day I worked as a full-time employee of the NHS.

For years after I left, the A&E department had several managers, none staying very long, mainly due to lack of support from senior management. The chief executive, Sue Jennings, was called before a government select committee to explain failings at the trust and in 2003/4, the director of finance, Alan Whittle, was appointed chief executive to replace her. By 2009, a report published by the Care Quality Commission concluded that lack of leadership contributed to an estimated 400 avoidable deaths in a year at Basildon. In 2013, the hospital was put into special measures and Alan Whittle resigned. I am glad I left when I did.

Since a new chief executive has taken over the hospital, it has greatly improved and was removed from special measures in 2014. The A&E department has been redesigned with a second floor (something I wanted but was told could not be provided because of the foundations). With the relocation of the endoscopy unit, the department has now taken back the space that was originally promised in 1990. Perhaps after 28 years since centralisation of A&E services and 27 years since the hospital became a trust, improvements are now underway.

As for Orsett Hospital, its fate was sealed in 1991. Despite all the promises that it was safe, beds were continually closed and parts of the unit downgraded. In 2004, the hospital was bulldozed to the ground and only a small part of the original unit remains for outpatients and day care. The Burma Star Association's memorial, that stood in the grounds of the hospital, remains in what is now Hew Watt close, part of the housing estate where once was a 500-bed hospital.

But I'm cheered by the fact that included in what is left of Orsett Hospital is the minor injuries unit. It is now a very important service to the community seeing over 200 patients a day. And providing this service are fully trained emergency nurse practitioners.

20 A NEW BEGINNING

When I awoke on the morning of 1st June 1992, I was not sure if I should consider myself to be on holiday or a self-employed person without any work. Of course, I had the regional role that would commence the following Monday. And I had a whole range of activities planned including teaching the student paramedics on Tuesday morning, an RCN meeting that evening, a Red Cross meeting on Wednesday and an A&E conference meeting on Thursday. On Friday and Saturday we had the Essex A&E conference, so there was plenty to sort out for that.

While considering how the next six months were going to pan out, I received a call from a senior manager at King's College Hospital, London. Would I be available to undertake a review of their A&E department and would I meet with him and other managers late Thursday afternoon to discuss the consultancy? My answer was: yes. In preparation for the meeting, I rang a self-employed colleague and asked: "How much do I charge?" Up to that point, I had not considered taking any work other than with the region and that fee had been set as if I was employed. When she suggested a figure, I was almost speechless. "Will they pay that per day?" I asked. "Yes," was the reply, "And that is at the lower end of the scale."

When I attended the meeting, I was asked to review the A&E department from a service perspective including staffing, management, records, patient flow and the general layout of the department. The manager was aware they had many problems including no designated waiting room as this had been turned into a clinical area to help resolve the increase in patient attendees. When I was taken on a visit to the department, I could not believe what I saw. This was going to be quite a challenge but one I relished. I quoted my daily rate, it was immediately accepted, and we agreed on a start date of 25th June.

My meeting with Kate Harmond at the regional offices in Paddington on Monday 8th June went well. I came away with a clear understanding of the work needed to make the regional A&E guidelines document a reality. Much of the work I could do at home but some required regular meetings at the regional office.

The first hurdle I had to overcome was how I was going to get the regional work typed? I also had an article for an A&E journal that needed typing up. So I decided to pay one of the hospital secretaries to do it. Knowing the length of the regional work, I vowed I would start teaching myself to type and use a word processor.

The regional project progressed well and I found I was working from 9am until about 3pm two to three days a week. Suddenly I was earning money again, enjoying what I was doing, and I had much more free time than when I was at Basildon. I had not been so happy since my days as a nursing officer at Orsett.

One recommendation from the regional guidelines that was taken up across the UK was a new system of hospital signage. During initial discussions, a number of us made the point that hospitals with or without A&E had the same signage. Kate

Harmond came up with the idea for new signs (with a white H and blue background for non-A&E hospitals and a red background for units with A&Es). Another key recommendation was the nurse staffing of A&E departments including using patient dependency as part of the staffing and skill mix review.

By the 27th July, I had produced the draft document and, like all publications, it went through a number of reviews and committees until it was finally published in the Autumn under the title Accident & Emergency Services – A Guide to Good Practice. I felt very proud that I had produced a document that was going to improve A&E services and, most importantly, improve the service to the patient. My first piece of work as a self-employed nurse consultant was complete.

The meeting on my first day at King's College A&E in June was an introduction to the task ahead. As this was the first review of an A&E I had ever undertaken, I was keen to impress. I prepared a structure for the consultancy including who I would wish to interview, the importance of spending time observing practice and getting staff to be open with me and share their ideas of how things could improve. My plan was well received and my first full day was on 14th July.

The A&E department at King's was located in the older part of the hospital. It was a small department and the patient volume was such that the waiting room had been re-designated as a clinical area. There was a separate children's facility and GPs, as well as A&E medical staff, worked alongside nurses and other health care staff. There was a focus on research and I met the nurse researcher, Robert Crouch, which proved to be the start of a working relationship between the pair of us that would last for many years.

As the waiting room was now a clinical area the only place for patients to sit was along the corridors. This proved to be very impractical because as trolleys moved up and down, patients had to constantly move their legs to avoid injury. The clinical waiting room was horrendous, with rows of stretcher trolleys in such a configuration that to provide any care to a patient in the centre meant several trolleys had to be moved to gain access. There were no curtains and no privacy. The trolleys were so close to each other that the sides touched. On the periphery of the room were clinical bays, so if a patient in the clinical waiting room needed to use a bedpan, the patient in the room would be moved out. Then the patient on the trolley would be moved in and, after using the bedpan, the whole process would be reversed.

To gain a perspective on what it was like to work in such an environment, I worked a few clinical shifts and, during one, a patient in the middle of the trolley area started to vomit. To reach them with a vomit bowl I had to move several other patients and, by this time, vomit was all over the trolley and the surrounding trolleys where the patients were not at all amused.

Overall, I spent 16 days visiting the department over several weeks and produced my final report in September. I was asked if I would undertake further work. This linked me with Rob Crouch and together we developed a number of improvements

to nursing documentation and nursing practice including the use
of the Model of Nursing developed at Orsett.

Coming back into central London after a consultancy day, I
would often eat in one of the riverside restaurants. As I sat
enjoying the summer evenings, I would reflect on whether
consultancy was something I could develop further, or should I
return to the NHS? One thing I liked about being self-employed
was that I could combine business with pleasure.

Feeling I needed some peer guidance on my future career, I met
with Tom Bolger, who I had known from cadet and student days
and who was now director of education at the RCN. I knew I
wanted to undertake further consultancy and also to develop
expert witness work and teaching. After a constructive
discussion with Tom, and after thinking hard about a whole
range of possibilities, I decided I would pursue a career as a self-
employed consultant, lecturer and expert witness, at least for
now. I purchased an Amstrad computer and thought I had really
moved into the modern age with my green screen, keyboard and
the ability to save my work on a floppy disc. Although it was
just an upmarket word processor, complete with a printer, it
would make my reports and student study notes look much
more professional. I would use the logo 'AccEm' from **Accident
& Emergency**. I felt my new career at last had some focus,
although it would take some time to become well and truly
established.

Having decided on a career plan I took the opportunity to travel
to Belgium in September as a pillion rider on a hardtail chopper

motorbike. I am not sure the lower half of my body ever recovered! The next day was the main ride through Brussels in protest at proposed European legislation for motorbikes. I have to confess I knew nothing about the politics of the event; I had just gone for a weekend away to hear the bands, enjoy the ride and meet new friends. I met many people including one named Ray and over the last 27 years he has become like a brother and his girlfriends have become friends of mine. Being a pillion rider inspired me to take motorbike lessons. Mum was horrified and told me: "I dreaded this might happen when you were 16. I didn't think you would be doing it at 40!" But I did and I passed.

Over several years, with many friends I met through the motorbike clubs, I attended further European events and local UK rallies. Unfortunately, in 1998, I was out on the M25 when a car knocked me off the bike. Following surgery to my hand and three days in hospital, I was discharged and I attended as an outpatient. I had to cancel several days' work but I was not put off riding. Once my hand was functional and I was able to pull the clutch lever I was back riding with my friends.

As chair of the RCN A&E Association, I continued to work to develop A&E nursing. Over my eight year period as chair, we ran conferences, study days and met with representatives from numerous health care organisations. Working groups were essential such as the one drawn from the British Association for Emergency Medicine and the RCN. Our remit was the production of guidance on bereavement care in A&E. During 1993 and 1994, we gathered evidence from over 200 organisations and visited individuals and departments. It was also the first and only time I have been swimming with a nun. The final document was published in March 1995.

Knowing my time as chair of the Association and of the Essex A&E group was ending in 1995, as well as my position on the Joint Royal Colleges Advisory Group for paramedic development, I decided to become a trustee of Essex Red Cross. With other trustees, we were accountable for the charity and the governance of the Red Cross at county level. I held this position until 1998 when the British Red Cross brought together the 84 individual charities into one unified organisation with a single national board of trustees. I also decided to stand for the RCN Council. I visited all the local branches, met as many members as possible during the early part of 1995 and gained enough backing for my election that when nominations were announced I was elected unopposed.

In October 1997, I was elected vice-chair of RCN Council for two years. This was extended for a further two years after my re-election in 1999. Taking on an honorary officer role increased my work commitment considerably. When the International Council of Nurses held its biannual conference in London in 1999, its centenary year, I attended the opening ceremony in the Albert Hall London. As vice-chair of council, with the deputy president, we hosted the four chief nursing officers of the UK and were allocated the royal box. From that vantage point we had a magnificent view of the proceedings and, as the flags of the nations were unfurled from the upper balconies, a kaleidoscope of colours unfolded around the hall.

I was also able to attend a lunch at Marlborough House in the presence of Her Majesty the Queen and had the pleasure of being introduced to her. As a Fellow of the Florence Nightingale Foundation (awarded by the foundation and presented by HRH Princess Alexandra in 1995), I was asked to join other fellows of the Foundation and the fellows of the RCN to form a procession at a Westminster Abbey service from the west end of the building to our places in the lantern. As we moved through the nave and choir areas hundreds of nurses from around the world were watching and I felt so proud that the UK was hosting such a prestigious event.

Princess Alexandra presenting me with my Fellowship of the Florence Nightingale Foundation in 1995

Photo: Raymond Irons

21 CALL THE EXPERT WITNESS

One advantage of being known through the RCN A&E Association was many nurse managers were happy to engage me for consultancy work. Over the next 12 years I reviewed A&E services in a number of hospitals throughout the UK. Some involved a review of all aspects of the A&E service while others were for a specific issue such as introducing triage or improving practice through improved ways of working. On some occasions, such as at Oldchurch Hospital and West Middlesex Hospital, I was invited to help with the implementation of the changes or was engaged for further work.

Staffing was becoming a very significant issue as under Project 2000 students moved from schools of nursing to university and to my mind became almost divorced from hospitals and the NHS. At the same time pupil nurse training ceased heralding the end of the enrolled nurse role. Although these changes were phased, what A&E departments were left with was the loss of the student nurse, pupil nurse, and enrolled nurse. At the same time there was an increase in the number of registered nurses and a substantial increase in ancillary staff whose name was changed from auxiliary to health care assistant (HCAs). Ironically in 2017 with the introduction of the three-year student nursing degree apprenticeship, and nursing associates who undertake a two-year education programme regulated by the Nursing & Midwifery Council, we seem to have come full circle.

It was also at this time that the full implications of reduced A&E departments and hospital beds were causing concern. In Essex alone we had three A&E departments close and all hospitals reduced bed numbers. When the political decision was made to cut beds, we had been told that community services would be improved. The reality was that beds were rapidly closed yet community services continue even today to play catch-up. Despite the massive reduction in the length of stay for most patients, especially surgical patients, there continues to be hundreds of patients across the UK each day waiting in emergency departments for a bed to become available.

What I came across repeatedly during my consultancy work was that in most departments, the staff had the answers to the problems, but senior management insisted on paying people like me to tell them what most of their staff already knew. This became even more apparent during 2009 when the Mid Staffs scandal broke. Peter Carter, the then general secretary of the Royal College of Nursing, said in a Nursing Standard article that year: 'Nurses raise concerns but no one listens.'

Not all my consultancy work involved reviewing A&E departments. At Dewsbury Hospital the work covered the whole unit and involved visiting the hospital two days a month for 18 months. I was working with senior ward nursing staff to develop their management and professional skills. I also worked with the director of nursing at the University of Essex on the development of an MSc course for A&E nursing and a similar but shorter consultancy at Bournemouth University. In Northern Ireland, I spent several months working with the university on the development of an MSc for disaster nursing.

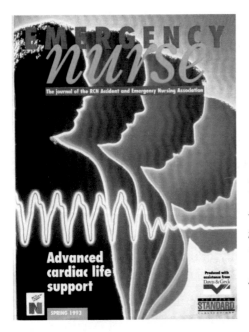

The very first issue of Emergency Nurse published in April 1993.
The journal proved to be a success

Front cover: RCNi

Meanwhile the editor of Nursing Standard engaged me to find sponsors for the Emergency Nurse supplement which led to the next phase of the journal's development, the production of a stand-alone 32-page journal launched in April 1993. Emergency Nurse proved such a success that in 2012 it celebrated 20 years of publication. I wrote an article for the celebratory edition entitled 'Two Decades of Change'.

Then in 1994 the Chief Nursing Officer (CNO) for England, Yvonne Moores, appointed me as her honorary consultant adviser in Accident & Emergency Nursing. I attended many meetings with civil servants, government ministers and others and undertook a major study of A&E services. I became a member of the Chief Medical Officer's working party on community emergency care.

The A&E study was a snapshot of A&E departments in the first three months of 1997. As I look back at the report 22 years on, although much has changed, many issues remain the same. This includes new attendances continuing to rise, especially in the number of medical and elderly patients, the increased dependency of patients and the extra work all this entails not being matched with additional funding. The report also demonstrated the continued increase in primary care patients with poor access to GP services, especially at weekends and nights. Nurse staffing was also an issue with many managers calling for a staffing and skill-mix formula to be available.

The Chief Medical Officer's report included several recommendations, one of which was an emergency telephone helpline that very soon became NHS Direct and remains as the advice line NHS 111.

Probably the most interesting pieces of work I undertook was for the Patient Charter Unit. The Charter came into effect on 1st April 1992. Although a number of rights and standards had a direct impact on A&E, Charter Standard 5 caused most controversy. This indicated that a patient would be seen immediately and the need for treatment assessed. Soon after publication, an audit time of five minutes was linked to the standard. I was appointed by the unit to undertake a review including visits to 44 A&E departments in England.

Throughout January – March 1995 I travelled the length and breadth of England. Some weeks I would travel to the north or west and be away for the week. I would be in my first hospital by 9am and by early afternoon I would be on the road to the next hospital, finishing at around 7pm and usually staying at a bed and breakfast near the hospital I planned to visit the following day.

As it was winter, I often had to battle the weather and no more so than my visits in the North-West. In late January, I had an appointment in Liverpool linked to my work as an expert witness and I was then visiting Wythenshawe hospital in Manchester the following day. As I left Liverpool, the snow was falling heavily and by the time I reached the M62 the outside lane was covered in thick snow. Driving in blizzard conditions, I arrived at the hotel near the hospital at 5.30pm. In my room, I switched on the local news to see the M62 just outside Liverpool closed, with cars trapped on the motorway. Next morning the news was full of stories from stranded motorists, some of whom had spent the night trapped in their cars. I was lucky to have left Liverpool when I did.

The visits to the A&E departments were revealing. Department managers were keen to assure me that the audit time of five minutes from arrival to nursing assessment was achieved in their department. In reality, it seldom was. In many departments, it took me five minutes to reach and speak to a receptionist so I knew it would be longer to see a nurse. In other departments, a nurse would see the patient first, but what became known as the 'hello nurse' was of very little benefit. It was more a way of simply ticking a box indicating the standard had been achieved.

During my visits, I would obtain information from both staff and patients. It was also important to write down their ideas so that the report contained a range of recommendations that came from all sources and not just me. My lasting memory from one patient interview was his words: "Don't tell us lies, tell us the truth." He pointed to the scrolling information sign on the waiting room wall. It said: 'waiting time for doctor 30 minutes'. But he told me: "I've been here an hour and still not seen a doctor." The patient went on to say he understood his injury was not serious, and he knew he was not a priority, but his message was that he did not want a false promise about the waiting time. What I learned from this major piece of work was that government moves slowly. It was not until May 1996 that draft papers were circulated with my main recommendations for a better quality initial assessment and a 15 minutes audit time.

* * *

Over the first 12 years, I provided a range of workshops and study days from monthly eye emergency lectures through to regular resuscitation workshops for all trust staff at South Essex Mental Health and Community Trust. In addition, having achieved registration from the Health and Safety Executive to run my own First Aid at Work courses, I expanded this part of the business and became the sole provider of such courses to the Port of Tilbury, one of the largest docks in the UK and the principal port for London. Adding to my portfolio, I started providing a series of study days for 3M Health Care and courses for M&K Updates.

Due to the development of Primary Care Trusts (PCTs) I was

now visiting health centres, care homes and community hospitals, providing training including venepuncture and cannulation, nursing records and resuscitation. Resusci Anne, Junior and Infant joined me on more car journeys than my family.

Another major work stream for me began after I started what became a regular monthly study day programme at Monklands, Scotland in 1994. Soon I was asked to run other such study days throughout the UK. I particularly enjoyed my visits to Monklands, especially the flight which included an excellent lunch with wine!

The study days on major incidents that I ran for Nursing Standard gave me an opportunity to use material from major events that had occurred in the 1980s. Using slides and videos, I drew common themes from incidents such as the Bradford football stadium fire, King's Cross underground fire, Hillsborough football stadium disaster, Clapham rail crash, the Kegworth and Lockerbie air disasters. On Saturday 15th June 1996 I was in Cardiff lecturing all day and closed off from what was happening in the world. So we had no idea that during the afternoon the IRA had set off a 1.5kg bomb in Manchester city centre. As I returned to meet instructor colleagues on the TNCC course running in Abergavenny I was met by a sea of devastated faces. When they told me the news, it felt ironic that all day I had been lecturing on how to deal with a major incident while 197 miles away one was happening for real. Two of the instructors were very distressed as both were from Manchester and one could not locate her mother while the other was unable to reach her husband. Neither knew if their loved ones had been in the city centre at the time. Fortunately, after some agonising hours, they were informed their family members were safe. Their concern could then turn to the fact that Marks and Spencer had been destroyed.

Probably one of the more important contacts I made during that time was Christina Machan, the county training and development manager for Buckinghamshire Primary Care Trust. With Christina and Sally McCornack (my colleague and friend from Orsett) we developed a long-running health care assistants course providing all the knowledge and skills that an HCA required when working in a GP surgery. The course was initially linked with Milton Keynes college so the HCAs obtained a National Vocational Qualification (NVQ) but then the Open University (OU) was so impressed they agreed to award a diploma. This also led to a similar course for therapy assistants.

One of the most rewarding aspects of the HCA course was seeing how individual HCAs developed. I recall one particular lady on the introductory day who was very shy and described herself as 'only the cleaner.' As the course progressed, we saw a transformation to a self-confident HCA. By the end this lady was a different person, full of confidence, debating with her peers. She continued to progress and ended up running several clinics independently within a GP surgery.

Sally and I also developed a course that enabled HCAs to administer certain vaccines and drugs. Although some work around this was developing in the UK, it was relatively new and very few, if any, courses existed. Having established the legal position and guidelines from the NHS to support general practice, we developed a six-week course and were pleased when it passed muster with the Health Protection Agency (part of the Department of Health). The course became so well established in Buckinghamshire, we ran it two to three times a year for a number of other NHS training companies.

Then in 2002 I was invited by the Singapore Emergency Nurses group to carry out a consultancy and lecture tour. I visited the university where all health care education is taught and attended several A&E departments presenting papers and meeting with medical, nursing and health officials. Although I found many nurses were highly trained and experienced, the development of the role was restricted, mainly because the people of Singapore considered nursing a low status occupation compared to medicine. Advancing emergency nursing practice would require a cultural as well as professional shift and while some medical staff were supportive, others were not. After an exhausting but exhilarating and productive tour, including presenting two papers at their joint medical and nursing conference, I had a week's holiday visiting tourist attractions and meeting up for dinner with many of the nurses.

* * *

My interest in expert witness work was stimulated by two incidents during my time as head of nursing services at Basildon. The first was when a man in his late 50s was brought into A&E after a large tree branch fell and pinned his leg to the ground.

Some passers-by eventually lifted the branch and an ambulance was called. The man's lower leg was bruised but the X-ray showed no fracture. A simple support bandage was applied and he was discharged. But the next morning he was brought in dead. The fatal error was no one asked how long the branch had been on his leg. Even as a Red Cross first aider I had always been taught not to remove a crushing object after 20 minutes otherwise deadly chemicals from the limb pass into the circulation and damage organs, especially the kidneys.

The second incident involved a patient who had an abscess drained from her armpit. The nurse left the cubicle because a patient nearby suffered a cardiac arrest. The surgical registrar, having completed the procedure, also left the cubicle without ensuring the woman's safety. The patient then fell from the trolley and fractured her hip. I advised the chief executive to admit that the hospital had failed in our duty of care and to accept liability.

The case that started my formal involvement in expert witness work also involved a patient who had (allegedly) fallen from a trolley. The case had been going on for many months without an outcome. When I read the case files, I formed the view that the patient had not fallen, but got off the trolley, and then fell. From the point of view of a risk assessment, this was significant. At the Royal Courts of Justice in the Strand, central London, just before we entered the courtroom, both barristers approached me for a final opinion. They then decided to settle out of court. The judge was very unhappy that having convened a court hearing, they had only now agreed to settle literally outside the courtroom doors.

Having decided expert witness work was for me, I attended two days of training. As an expert witness, irrespective of who engaged me, it was essential that I remained independent and my report reflected this. Over the next 12 years, I undertook a number of cases, many involved alleged negligence by nurses in A&E and often they centred on a patient falling off a trolley, or getting off a trolley and falling. Other cases involved alleged inadequate observation of the patient resulting in deterioration of their condition.

One incident involved a doctor in a pre-hospital situation stopping resuscitation. I made it clear to the solicitor that I was an A&E nurse expert, not a doctor. The solicitor was happy because of my knowledge of trauma and asked me to give an opinion. After reading the post-mortem report, and having reviewed various trauma scoring systems to calculate the probability of survival, it was clear that the patient would not have survived. So I agreed that the doctor was right to stop the resuscitation.

The case where a nurse claimed that an injury she sustained was due to the trust failing to provide appropriate equipment was an interesting one. It involved the removal of a blade from a scalpel handle. As it was a complicated case for the legal team, I was asked to demonstrate the correct use of the equipment in front of a panel of solicitors and barristers from both sides. They concluded that whilst I demonstrated the safe method of removing the blade, and whilst it might be the traditional method used in many hospitals, they could see the potential risks. Sadly like most cases, I never heard the outcome.

I was asked to give my view on the possible misdiagnosis and discharge of a patient who, hours later, suffered a cardiac arrest and died. I was concerned that the nurse's statement suggested she might have questioned the doctor's decision to send the patient home. So I met with the nurse to hear her version of events and her knowledge of the test results. It was clear that nothing the nurse did, or did not do, had any bearing on the subsequent death.

In another case a nurse had used an incorrect cleaning solution on a patient's wound. A commonly used solution was supplied as a surgical scrub or alcohol solution. Both bottles were almost identical and the nurse had used the wrong solution. Although she was in the wrong, I did point out that the manufacturers should consider changing the design of the bottles and this was taken into account when the case was concluded.

At one hospital I encountered an attempt to make A&E staff a scapegoat for others' negligence. A lady had a chest drain inserted in the A&E department. On arrival on the ward, everything was fine, but shortly afterwards bleeding was observed from the drain site and complications set in. The claim was inadequate post-insertion observation of the drain site by A&E nurses. As I pointed out in the report, until the lady was in the ward there was no problem so the deterioration could hardly be down to A&E staff.

In similar vein a relative claimed the A&E triage nurse had not recorded significant history which meant the doctor did not make a correct diagnosis. The nurse insisted the relative had not conveyed the information claimed yet the relative insisted she had. My conclusion was that it was one person's word against another's, yet why doubt the nurse who had no reason not to record something significant if she had been told. These cases are very difficult and often it's a matter of making a judgement call.

Another case involved a nurse who had sustained injuries that prevented a return to work and part of the compensation claim was to gain sufficient income for the rest of his life. The solicitor asked me to speculate on what a nurse, who had just qualified, would be earning, and at what grade, if they had been able to continue in the profession for the next 10-20 years. I reported that so much depended on the individual it was impossible to say how far the nurse would have progressed on the career ladder. I offered a series of scenarios and then it was up to the solicitor and others to determine what they considered reasonable.

My final case was yet another instance where a patient had climbed off a trolley and fallen. The case had been going on for years and was so controversial the expert witness for the patient's solicitors and I were asked to meet together and come up with an agreed joint report. Both of us laid out our areas of concern and we identified areas we both agreed on, and those we did not. It was then a matter of trying to reach a compromise on the areas of disagreement. After six hours of intense discussion, we did reach an agreed report and the case was finally closed out of court.

22 PIECING THE JIGSAW TOGETHER

In 1996 the local university in my area advertised a part-time post for a lecturer/practitioner to run a postgraduate A&E course. This seemed an ideal way to continue my enjoyment of teaching while still having time for self-employed work. I was one of a small number of interviewees, all of whom I knew, and I was aware I was the most experienced and had held more senior positions than they had. During the interview, I was getting the distinct feeling that the senior tutor felt threatened by my experience, implying that I would have difficulty being managed. As I predicted, I was unsuccessful.

But this led me to focus on my future direction. I believed that I could continue to support myself financially with the work I was getting from consultancy, lecturing and expert witness work. It was probably the first time it dawned on me I had built a business made up of many small activities. It was like a jigsaw in which all the pieces were important, but if one piece dropped away there would be another to fill that gap. It was also time for me to expand.

My local newspaper, the Thurrock Gazette, was encouraging businesses to apply for the annual Thurrock Business Awards in 2000. All entrants would have one free advertisement in the paper and success would mean further publicity. Although I did not expect to win, I decided to apply and at least get some free advertising. The awards dinner was held in June 2000 at the Civic Hall. I was so convinced I stood no chance I almost did not attend. Fortunately I decided to go and took Mum as my guest.

I was a winner at the Thurrock Business Awards

To my surprise my name was called and I was delighted to receive a plaque and a framed copy of the article about me that had appeared in the Gazette. I also knew that my business would now be advertised in the paper the following week as one of the winners. Entering the awards twice more over the next five years, I was fortunate to win the award on both occasions.

During the early summer of 2001, I was asked if I would provide nursing cover to a group of disabled adults for a coach holiday to Germany. It included a tour of Cologne, Dresden, a visit to Colditz Castle and many beautiful mountain passes and lakes.

Needless to say I agreed and early on in the holiday, one of the guests did not appear for breakfast. I knew the man had diabetes and when I asked the hotel staff to open his bedroom door I found him in a hypoglycaemic coma. While we waited for the ambulance, I maintained his airway and as I rubbed glucose on his lips he began to regain consciousness. The ambulance paramedics administered glucose and he was taken to the hospital and was released the same day. Fortunately, that was the only emergency and I had a very nice holiday with the group.

In the following year the holiday in Austria demanded more of my nursing skills. One lady known to have Parkinson's disease was taking her medication and one of the side effects is what is called the on-off syndrome. Literally, the person can be walking and talking one minute, then lose all power in the limbs, and appear quite blank. For a couple of days, the guest required a wheelchair and help with eating and drinking.

The evening before the end of the holiday, the guest who had suffered a hypoglycaemic attack the previous year did so again. In the packed hotel restaurant, he started swaying about on his chair and shouting. I went over and tried to persuade him to drink some glucose water but he was having none of it. Suddenly he threw himself on the floor and started crawling around on all fours. I put a handful of glucose powder in my hand, chased him across the floor and literally pushed it into his mouth. With him spitting and me almost riding on his back the scenario continued for some minutes. Suddenly he stopped and said: "You were right. I was hypo. Can I get up now?" I suggested he had a drink of the glucose water then we could both get to our rooms to clean up. With both of us, and the restaurant floor, covered in glucose powder, I am sure the hotel staff and other guests will not forget that evening's entertainment.

* * *

Becoming a Fellow of The Royal College of Nursing was a great honour, although the way I heard about it was rather unusual. At an RCN Council meeting in 2002, an item to discuss new Fellows was on the agenda after tea on the first afternoon. I realise now I was deliberately delayed at tea by staff members,

Receiving my RCN Fellowship in 2002.
The citation highlighted the Jones
Dependency Tool I developed
Photo: RCN

and as I returned to the meeting everyone clapped and laughed. I had no idea what was going on until the President passed me the agenda item on a separate page saying: "Now you can have the full list of the proposed Fellows we have just approved." And on the list was my name.

My fellowship was awarded for services to emergency nursing and in the citation it highlighted the development of the Jones Dependency Tool and my involvement with the RCN Faculty of Emergency Nursing. The dependency tool, designed at Orsett back in the 1980s and used on a number of occasions during my consultancy work, was modified, validated and shown to be transferable and recommended for the measurement of adult patient dependency in the emergency department in 2001.

My former colleague Rob Crouch, with his principal project researcher Susan Williams, published their findings that year and it was at this stage Rob named the tool the Jones Dependency Tool (JDT). I wrote a chapter on it for a jointly edited book produced by Rob, Ruth Endacott and myself. Entitled Emergency Nursing Care Principles and Practice it was published in 2003. The JDT is now used in the UK, and in many other countries, particularly in Portugal. In 2014 I was invited to meet with senior nurses from emergency care in Portugal and speak at their international conference. I also visited two emergency departments where the JDT is in use. In 2015, I presented a joint paper with the Portuguese A&E nurses at the International Council of Nurses (ICN) conference in South Korea. The RCN Emergency Care Association has incorporated the JDT as one of the key measurements in the Baseline

Emergency Staffing Tool (BEST).

The Faculty of Emergency Nursing (FEN) was the brainchild of Rob Crouch and in collaboration with numerous emergency nurses (and me) it was launched at RCN Congress in April 2003. By autumn 2005, the FEN was going from strength to strength with 1,200 affiliated nurses. At the 2006 A&E conference Jill Windle, as chair of FEN, presented me with the first Honorary Fellowship of the Faculty of Emergency Nursing. Using a quote from a commemorative plaque by Su Andi on Salford Quays, "From the labour of yesterday lives the spirit of tomorrow," Jill highlighted my work in emergency nursing and for the Faculty. As I stepped forward to receive the certificate, I was lost for words as several hundred emergency nurses rose to give me a standing ovation.

Despite the success of the Faculty, changes within the nursing structure of the RCN in 2006 led to it becoming an independent body. Although it has not become the lead in emergency nursing that both Rob and I envisaged, FEN continues to play a role in the speciality. Its philosophy has greatly influenced the RCN's accreditation of advanced nurse practitioners and the RCN Emergency Care Association's National Curriculum and Competency Framework for emergency nurses. Had the Faculty concept continued, the RCN would be 11 years ahead of the game.

The RCN A&E Association held its second international conference in 2000 and 26 nurses, each representing a different country, signed a Declaration of Friendship. Following a discussion on international co-operation, we were offered the opportunity of a web page on the International Council of Nurses website. The declaration would be published and each organisation would add some information on the web page and it would become the tool to maintain international links without the bureaucracy of a formal organisation.

Benny Marett, the 2000 president of the Emergency Nurses Association USA asked me to visit their conference in Chicago that autumn and present the concept of the declaration and web site to US emergency nurses. A meeting of the International Council of Nurses in Copenhagen in 2001 followed where I chaired the inaugural two-hour meeting with representatives from the UK, Cyprus, Denmark, Greece, Italy, Jamaica, Taiwan, Seychelles, South Africa, Sweden and the US.

23 NEW NAME, NEW BEGINNING

In 2004 I decided it was time for a change of business focus. Although I would continue with emergency care training it was no longer appropriate for me to continue the expert witness work, or to be going into A&E departments as an emergency nursing specialist. Thurrock Enterprise Agency offered business advice and I had joined the monthly small business club some years earlier. Meeting with Graeme Loveland, manager and advisor for the agency, I discussed my last 12 years in business and my thoughts for the future. His advice was invaluable in helping me focus on my business development and the need to change its name. AccEm was linked entirely to Accident & Emergency, yet my business encompassed far more and had developed almost entirely into training and development.

I chose the name Health Care Training and Development Services as this encompassed professional, clinical and first aid at work courses and better reflected the work I was now undertaking. The business became a limited company in 2006, and due to its growth, I registered for VAT in 2007. By now I had a number of instructors working with me, some of whom ran their own business while others had a range of part-time training jobs with other companies.

I also briefly returned to clinical practice. Gerard Cronin, the Nurse Manager at Basildon A&E, drew up a contract whereby I worked unpaid in the department so that I could maintain clinical credibility in emergency care.

I designed a half-day workshop for South Essex Mental Health Trust nursing staff on how to teach basic resuscitation. This enabled the trust to comply with national guidelines incorporating resuscitation training within control and restraint training. Following this, I designed and taught a two-day enhanced emergency care course enabling mental health nurses to better deal with physical emergencies. I also provided 'train the trainer' workshops to health visitors in Thurrock who are required to teach care of next infant (CONI) resuscitation to parents who have lost a child due to Sudden Infant Death Syndrome.

Although I won three business awards and built a thriving company, that did not stop me from making a wrong decision to work for a doctor. She was a locum at a local trust and ran a company providing training for overseas doctors who wished to register with the General Medical Council and then practise in the UK. She asked me to provide a number of study days, each including resuscitation, advisory defibrillation and trauma assessment and intervention.

Having agreed on the training dates during May and June 2005, I expected to arrive at a purpose-built training venue. Instead, I was sent to a terraced house in East Ham, East London, and found a make-shift room made of ply-wood which filled the garden. A number of men arrived - many appeared to be living in the house. They came from a range of countries and, as the day progressed, I began to wonder if some of them had ever qualified as doctors. If the doctor who had engaged me had not appeared at the end of the day I am sure I would not have continued with this work. The next training day was at the same venue with a new group of men and while some knew the basics of what I was teaching, others appeared baffled by what was simple information.

The third training day began with my discovery that the house appeared to be empty apart from one man who informed me the venue had changed. He directed me to another house where at least the training room was now within the building. The men who attended appeared more knowledgeable than those from the previous sessions. In fact I enjoyed teaching this group of doctors. But returning on the fourth day the house was empty, the organising doctor's mobile phone was disconnected and no further contact was achieved. Fortunately, I had been paid for the first two days, but despite numerous attempts to contact the organising doctor no payment was forthcoming for the third day or my wasted journey on the fourth.

In 2002, my Aunty Eileen died and in 2004 I lost Mum. Both had been unwell for some time and while I always knew the day would come, it was nevertheless a blow for both my sister Jackie and myself. Having already suffered the loss of our nan and grandad and of course Dad in the 1990s, these latest losses brought an end to that close extended family I had always known.

I pressed on with my work as an RCN activist. Along with many other of the fellows I felt the contribution we could make to the RCN could improve significantly and this led to me being elected as Convenor of RCN Fellows in October 2005. I received a number of congratulatory letters including one from Baroness Cox who invited me to visit her in the House of Lords and I took up this invitation on 28th June 2006. As I sat watching the comings and goings, the lobby bell rang. Within seconds, people appeared from corridors and suddenly standing immediately in front of me was Baroness Margaret Thatcher, plus a number of her past cabinet colleagues from her time as Prime Minister while to my left I spotted Lord Neil Kinnock. All were almost within touching distance and for a moment I felt I was in a Tardis catapulted back to the 1980s.

Working with the Fellows' co-ordinating committee and two RCN staff members we devised a plan of action and, by using regular newsletters, encouraged many Fellows to re-engage with RCN activities. In 2006, it was the 30th anniversary of the RCN Fellows. We organised a celebratory dinner to link with the RCN annual meeting. Every Fellow was presented with a personalised copy of a booklet entitled Celebrating Excellence commemorating 30 years of RCN Fellowship. In my introduction I laid out our mission statement. I recognised that, like so much in nursing, there is nothing we were doing now, or will probably do in the future, that has not already been discussed, noted, agreed and in some cases actioned by past Fellows.

I remained the Convener until 2010 and during those five years the Fellows were energised. We had a regular slot at RCN Congress, we linked with a whole range of RCN work and held a one-day conference plus some very important meetings that influenced nursing and healthcare in the UK. Towards the end of my tenure RCN Council proposed another change to the governance structure. I had to defend the Fellows' position and our ability to influence. I am pleased to say we were successful and the Fellows continue to provide an excellent service to the RCN.

On 1st June 2012 I had been in business for 20 years and to celebrate I organised a black tie dinner and dance. I could not believe that two decades had passed since I left Basildon Hospital, especially as I had only intended staying out of the NHS for six months. My guests included my former cadet tutor June James, many people from my days at Orsett Hospital plus others who had helped me make my business a success.

On 30th July 2014 I had been a registered nurse for exactly 40 years and although I was still enjoying teaching, I felt it was time to review my work-life balance. I had enjoyed some marvellous holidays over recent years, including watching sunset and sunrise over Hawaii, and riding a Harley Davidson motorbike across the Golden Gate Bridge in San Francisco and down the Las Vegas strip in Nevada with my friend Ray, so I was keen for more 'downtime'. I was also tired of teaching every day then coming home to all the office work and the continuous preparation of student handouts plus sorting the bookings. It was time to look for a personal assistant and to focus on what I really wanted to teach, rather than what I was ending up teaching. I achieved both and my personal workload reduced considerably. It also allowed for such adventures as flying a tiger moth plane over Essex and a microlight over the Victoria Falls in Zambia.

By 2016 it was decision time about the business. I offered to sell it to Ian and Tina (two of the instructors) and they were delighted to take it on. I revalidated with the NMC in July giving me a further three years of registration to practise as a Registered Nurse. Knowing I wanted to celebrate 25 years in business, the sale went ahead on 1st June 2017. I organised a lunch on 31st May to thank the instructors and some of our key business contacts. Then in June I hosted a dinner/dance to celebrate with many friends from A&E, from my broader nursing life, with my sister and other friends attending.

During those 2017 celebrations, I could not help but reflect on my near 50 years in healthcare. The NHS I joined in 1969 was a far less complicated structure than it is today. It was a service managed by local management committees and within the hospital; the medical, nursing and administrative staff managed the day-to-day provision of care. But the move from a service to a business in the mid-1980s, then the internal market, purchaser/provider split and the introduction of NHS trusts all encouraged competition and a focus on finance which I felt overshadowed the quality of care.

Yet despite these more recent changes, my over 40 years in emergency nursing has seen dramatic improvements in patient care. The development of trauma care, trauma units, qualified trauma nurses through TNCC, and the rise of the paramedic service has improved the chance of survival for patients. Nurses have advanced their skills, developed emergency nurse practitioner roles, enhanced assessment and diagnostic skills as well as increasing many clinical skills that benefit patient care.

Triage and nursing documentation are standard practice in all emergency departments now.

Having sold the business in 2017, over the next two years I provided some training for Ian and Tina (the new owners of Health Care Training & Development Services Ltd.), continued as an instructor for the TNCC course and took a number of holidays including a world cruise at the start of 2019.

What the future holds for me is anybody's guess but I doubt I will be embarking on a new career. As David Cameron put it at his final Prime Minister's Questions: 'I was the future once'!

Sailing into the future... who knows what it holds for me?

LAST WORD

I finish where I began. The post arrived at about 7am each morning and on 15th May 2003, like any other morning, I quickly opened the letters before rushing out to work. Not paying attention to the envelope, I opened one letter and, as I glanced down, I saw it was from 10 Downing Street and signed by the Secretary for Appointments. It read:

> Dear Sir, The Prime Minister has asked me to inform you, in strict confidence, that he has it in mind, on the occasion of the forthcoming list of Birthday Honours, to submit your name to the Queen with a recommendation that Her Majesty may be graciously pleased to approve that you be appointed a Commander of the Order of the British Empire.

It went on to explain the procedure between receiving the letter and the Honours List being published. It also requested that, if I was agreeable to receiving the Honour, I should complete the enclosed form and send it back by return of post. I ticked yes in the box and dashed to the post box on the way to work. Now all I had to do was wait until 14th June and check that my name made it to the Honours List.

As midnight approached on 13th June, I had all the likely websites open ready for the list to appear. I checked them just after midnight but there was nothing. I switched from one site to the other until at 12.15am I found the published list on the BBC website. I scanned the names and there it was: 2003 Commanders of the Order of the British Empire, Gary Jones - For Services to

Emergency Nursing (Grays Essex). Not only was I delighted that my name appeared but also that it was specifically for services to emergency nursing. I could now tell everyone what I had been keeping secret for five long weeks.

During the early autumn I was notified by St. James's Palace that my investiture would be held on 25th November. I received my Warrant of Appointment, signed by the Queen, and as Grand Master of the Order, by Prince Philip. I then received a letter from the Garter Principal King of Arms of the College of Arms. He indicated that, as a CBE, I was eligible to petition for a grant of armorial bearings. What this meant was that I could have a personal coat of arms. I decided I would. I first had to send a

Outside Buckingham Palace after my investiture, with my sister Jackie, Mum and best friend Raymond Hicks
Photo: Charles Green

request to the Duke of Norfolk, Earl Marshal of England, who grants permission for armorial bearings on behalf of the Queen. I was then assigned a herald and between us, we designed my armorial bearings.

I wanted a crest that depicted my family, Orsett Hospital, Thurrock, the RCN and my link with the Florence Nightingale Foundation. For my family, we used an oak tree as my Nan and Grandad's address was Oak Road and this linked all of Mum's family. As Dad was a carpenter, an oak tree was appropriate for that side of the family too.

If you haven't already guessed, my family is very important to me. Both my parents served in the war, Mum in the RAF and Dad in the Navy. Once it all ended, they met at a local pub (the Orsett Cock) and married in July 1949. My sister was born 19 months after me and we are very close.

My grandparents on Mum's side were local, both having been born in Grays. For me, Oak Road was my second home. Both my grandparents were born in the early 1900s and they reflected the social positions of their time. Aunty Eileen, Mum's younger sister, never married and lived at home with Nan and Granddad. There is no doubt that Aunty being single gave her the opportunity to become a major part of my sister's and my upbringing.

Having agreed on the oak tree to represent my family, for Orsett Hospital we used the figure on my nurse's hospital badge. For the RCN I chose the stars and the sun from the RCN's Armorial

Bearings representing 24-hour care. For Florence Nightingale, a Turkish lamp, the type she would have used during her rounds in the Barrack Hospital at Scutari during the Crimean War. A dark blue wavy line across the shield represented the Thames, part of the Thurrock armorial bearings. The motto Experto Crede, in English reads Believe one who speaks from experience. I also had my CBE insignia incorporated into the design. In a sense my Coat of Arms reflects my whole life journey - my pathway to honour. My armorial motto sums it up: Believe me. I speak from experience.